# INTRODUCTORY
# LOGIC

*Third Edition*
*Revised and Expanded*

*Douglas J. Wilson*
*James B. Nance*

Canon Press

MOSCOW, IDAHO

## The Mars Hill Textbook Series

Introductory Logic, Doug Wilson & James B. Nance
Introductory Logic: Video Tapes featuring James B. Nance
Introductory Logic: Teacher Training Video Tapes featuring James B. Nance

Intermediate Logic, James B. Nance
Intermediate Logic: Video Tapes featuring James B. Nance
Intermediate Logic: Teacher Training Video Tapes featuring James B. Nance

Latin Primer: Book I, Martha Wilson
Latin Primer I: Video Tapes featuring Julie Garfield
Latin Primer I: Audio Pronunciation Tape featuring Julie Garfield

Latin Primer: Book II, Martha Wilson
Latin Primer II: Video Tapes featuring Julie Garfield
Latin Primer II: Audio Pronunciation Tape featuring Julie Garfield

Latin Primer: Book III, Martha Wilson
Latin Primer III: Video Tapes featuring Julie Garfield
Latin Primer III: Audio Pronunciation Tape featuring Julie Garfield

Latin Grammar: Book I, Doug Wilson & Karen Craig
Latin Grammar: Book II, Karen Craig

Matin Latin Book I, Karen Craig
Matin Latin Flashcards Book I, Karen Craig
Matin Latin Worksheet Pkt. Book I, Karen Craig
Matin Latin I: Video Tapes featuring Karen Craig

Matin Latin Book II, Karen Craig
Matin Latin Flashcards Book II, Karen Craig
Matin Latin Worksheet Pkt. Book II, Karen Craig
Matin Latin II: Video Tapes featuring Karen Craig

Douglas J. Wilson & James B. Nance, Introductory Logic
©1997 by Douglas J. Wilson & James B. Nance
Published by Canon Press, P.O. Box 8729, Moscow, ID 83843
800-488-2034 http://www.canonpress.org

First Edition 1997 (Rev. 2002)

Printed in the United States of America

ISBN: 1-885767-36-6

# Table of Contents

# Introduction

God created man with the ability to reason. He did this so that we could communicate with each other and so that we could obey Him. Reason allows us to form rational statements, and understand the statements of others. It allows us, for example, to take universal statements such as "God has commanded all men everywhere to repent," and apply them, first to ourselves, and then to our neighbor. Without the ability to reason, we would be unable to talk, preach, read, or follow God's commands.

Logic is the science and the art of reason. As a science, logic identifies the rules by which we reason. As an art it teaches how to follow those rules. About sixteen centuries ago, Augustine said this about the science of logic.

> *And yet the validity of logical sequences is not a thing devised by men, but is observed and noted by them that they may be able to learn and teach it; for it exists eternally in the reason of things, and has its origin with God. For as the man who narrates the order of events does not himself create that order; and as he who describes the situations of places, or the natures of animals, or roots, or minerals, does not describe arrangements of man; and as he who points out the stars and their movements does not point out anything that he himself or any other man has ordained; in the same way, he who says, "When the consequent is false, the antecedent must also be false," says what is most true; but he does not himself make it so, he only points out that it is so* (Augustine of Hippo, *On Christian Doctrine*, Book II, Chapter 32).

Logic is not devised by man, but neither is it created by God, like trees and stars are. Rather, it is an attribute of God which is reflected in creation. We see it primarily reflected in the minds of people. When we study logic, we study some of that reflection.

There are many different branches of formal logic. Two main branches are induction and deduction. Induction deals with arguments of likelihood and probability. It draws conclusions from specific facts or experience, conclusions which go beyond the facts. Inductive conclusions are never certain; they are either strong or weak, though they may be strengthened by further observation. Thus induction is the logic of the experimental sciences.

Deduction deals with arguments that are valid or invalid. If valid, the conclusions follow from the premises, and they do so with certainty. This book is an introduction to deductive logic. It covers topics such as statements and their relationships, syllogisms and validity, arguments in normal English, and informal fallacies.

# STATEMENTS AND THEIR
# RELATIONSHIPS

## Statements

In logic, as in other subjects, it is best to begin with the basic building blocks. In this subject, the basic building block is called a statement.

A **statement** is a particular kind of sentence. This sentence brings a message which can be said to be *either* true or false. Here is an example of a true statement:

*The apostle Paul wrote the book of Galatians.*

But statements can also be false. Here is an example:

*The apostle Paul wrote the book of Isaiah.*

In evaluating statements, we should be looking for their **truth value**. The first statement above has a *true* truth value. The second sentence is said to have a *false* truth value. If a sentence has *no* truth value, then it is not a statement at all. The following are *not* statements:

*Who wrote the book of 1 Timothy?*

*Husbands, love your wives as Christ loved the church.*

The first sentence is a question, and consequently has no truth value. It is neither true nor false, and therefore is not a statement.

The second sentence is a command. It also has no truth value, and is not a statement.

There is another kind of sentence that requires a little more care. It has the form of a statement, but it is not a real statement. Again, the instrument used to determine this is whether the sentence has a true or false truth value. For example:

*The round square furiously kicked the green yellowish.*

This looks like a statement, but it cannot even be said to be false. It doesn't refer to anything. It is best described as *nonsense*. Another example of nonsense is this:

*This statement is false.*

Is this true? Then it is false, and therefore true. Is it false? It is therefore true, and consequently false. Again, there is no real truth value here. This sentence cannot be identified as either true or false. It is therefore not a statement, at least not the kind of statement which we can legitimately use in logic.

**Summary:** A statement is a sentence which is either true or false. Other kinds of sentences which have no truth value—such as questions, commands, and nonsense—are not statements.

## The Laws of Thought

The fact that *any statement is either true or false* is one of the three basic laws of thought, upon which much of logic is based. This law of thought is called **The Law of Excluded Middle**, because it excludes the possibility of a truth value falling somewhere in the middle between true and false. Statements are either one or the other. If a statement is not true, then it is false, and vice versa.

Another fundamental law is called **The Law of Identity**. This law simply states that *if a statement is true then it is true*. A statement does not change its truth value if moved to a different place or time. This law may be employed to answer the unbeliever who says, "Christianity may be true for you, but not for me." No. If Christianity is true, then it is true.

The third law says that *a statement cannot be both true and false*. This is called **The Law of Noncontradiction**. Without this law, we could not argue for the exclusive truth of any statement which we hold. We could try to assert, for example, that "Jesus is God." But our opponents could respond, "Oh, I agree that what you say is true. But it is also false." We see that if we deny these laws, we lose the possibility of all logical reasoning.

**Summary:** Logic is based on three laws of thought. The Law of Identity says that if a statement is true, then it is true. The Law of Excluded Middle says that a statement is either true or false. The Law of Noncontradiction says that a statement cannot be both true and false.

## Statements and Their Relationships

### Exercise One

Examine the following sentences and determine whether or not they are statements. In the space provided, write down true statement, false statement, question, command, or nonsense. Be careful.

1. Jesus healed blind men. _True statement_

2. King David was the first king of Israel. _True statement_

3. The tongues of flame at Pentecost were water. _False statement_

4. Who wrote the book of Hebrews? _question_

5. Children, obey your parents. _command_

6. The Bible is the Word of God. _true statement_

7. The Great Pyramid is six feet high. _False statement_

8. Who said slaves should obey their masters? _question_

9. How old was Jesus when He was baptized? _question_

10. The slithy toves did gyre and gimble. _nonsense_

11. Believe the good news. _command_

12. The United States has fifty states. _True statement_

**Brain teaser:** God does not exist. _False statement_

## Self-supporting Statements

Once we have determined that a sentence is a statement, a further distinction can be made, the distinction between **self-supporting statements** and **supported statements**. This distinction depends upon the means by which the truth value of the statement is determined.

We will begin with self-supporting statements. Self-supporting statements are statements which have immediately apparent truth values. We do not need to consider information outside of the statements to determine their truth values. Self-supporting statements can be divided into three categories:

1. **Self-reports**. A self-report is a statement by a person concerning his own desires, beliefs or feelings. We usually do the charitable thing and take such a statement as true. For example:

*I believe that Jesus is the Son of God.*

The statement refers to the belief of the speaker; it does not primarily refer to whether Jesus is in fact the Son of God. In other words, the statement could be taken as true, even if Christianity were false. An atheist can acknowledge that it is true that the speaker *believes* that Jesus is the Son of God.

2. **Statements which are true or false by logical structure**. This is a statement which can be seen to be true or false by how the sentence is put together. For example:

*Jesus is the Son of God, or He is not.*

This statement is *necessarily* true. It cannot be false, because it covers all the possibilities. A statement which is true by logical structure is called a **tautology**. Other statements are necessarily false. For example:

*Jesus is the Son of God, and He is not the Son of God.*

This is an example of a **self-contradiction**, a statement which is false by logical structure.

3. **Statements which are true or false by definition.** Some statements are necessarily true or false because of the definitions of the words in the sentence. For example:

*All triangles are three-sided figures.*

This is necessarily true—it is true by definition. The following example is a statement which is false by definition.

*This triangle is an octagon.*

According to the definitions of *triangle* and *octagon*, the statement is necessarily false.

**Summary:** Self-supporting statements are statements for which we need no outside evidence to determine their truth value. There are three types of self-supporting statements: self-reports, statements which are true or false by logical structure, and statements which are true or false by definition.

## Exercise Two

1.  List below five examples of a phrase which would introduce a self-report, such as, "In my opinion..."

Wal-mart chiken is good.

Abortion is wrong.

My mom is brave.

Maureens got a bad attitude.

Tom needs hearing aids.

2.  List below five statements of your own which are true or false by logical structure. Include at least one tautology and one self-contradiction.

Maureens face is long, and is short.

Food is a necessity, or it is not

Paddy is Fat, or she is not.

Crackers are edible, and they are poisisas.

Felt is soft, and hard

3.  List below five statements which are true or false by definition.

Cheese is a meat product.

Microwaves heat food.

Kimonos are worn by Japanese folk.

Salt is a mineral we eat.

Russian is a language spoken by mexicans.

## Supported Statements

The other kind of statement is called a **supported statement**. A supported statement does not stand or fall by itself. It requires evidence from outside investigation before it can be declared true or false. Below are three examples of supported statements.

*Solomon had a treaty with Hiram.*

*It is raining outside.*

*The leaning tower will fall down.*

These are obviously statements; they are not questions or commands, and they can be said to be either true or false. But in order to determine the truth value of the statement, it is necessary to go *outside* the statement. We must gather some evidence before declaring them to be either true or false.

All the different types of statements we have studied so far can thus be organized into the following chart.

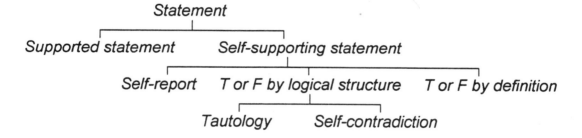

**Summary:** Self-supporting statements can be found to be true or false without looking beyond the sentence. Supported statements require one to collect evidence in order to determine their truth value.

**Exercise Three**

Examine each of the following statements. In the blank at the right, enter the type of statement you believe it to be. Your options are *self-report*, *self-supporting by logical structure*, *self-supporting by definition*, and *supported*.

1. *The snow is deep.*  _____

2. *I think Jesus is not what He claimed.*  _____

3. *Paul was an apostle, or he wasn't.*  _____

4. *Jericho fell to the invading Israelites.*  _____

5. *I believe David really loved Bathsheba.*  _____

6. *A square has four sides.*  _____

7. *The book of Genesis has fifty chapters.*  _____

8. *Jesus is God, and He is not God.*  _____

9. *Jesus is God, and He is man.*  _____

10. *I think the snow is deeper than last year.*  _____

11. *Jeremiah was a reluctant prophet.*  _____

12. *My mother is a woman.*  _____

13. *It either works, or it doesn't.*  _____

14. *Herod was an evil tyrant.*  _____

15. *The New Testament was written in Greek.*  _____

## Relationships Between Statements

We now need to examine some **relationships** between statements. Self-supporting statements and supported statements both can be related to other statements in many different ways. There are four major relationships with which we are concerned.

1. **Consistency:** When two statements can be true at the same time, we say they are consistent. For example, these two statements are consistent.

*Paul was an apostle.*

*The apostle Paul was never in Germany.*

These statements are consistent because there is no conflict between them. Consequently, they can both be true at the same time. If there is a conflict between the statements, then they are *inconsistent*. For an example of inconsistency, we may consider these:

*The apostle Paul was never in Germany.*

*The apostle Paul spent his life in Germany.*

It is not possible for both these statements to be true. If he was never in Germany, then he could not have spent his life there. The statements are therefore inconsistent.

2. **Implication:** Two statements are related by implication when the truth of the first requires or necessitates the truth of the second. If statement *P* implies statement *Q*, and if statement *P* is true, then statement *Q* must also be true. The following is an example of an implication.

*P: All Christians are followers of Jesus Christ.*

*Q: Some Christians are followers of Jesus Christ.*

He who says *P*, must also say *Q*. This is because *P* implies *Q*. It would not be possible for someone to maintain that all Christians were followers of

Christ, but that on the other hand some were not.

Many students of logic get confused over the use here of the word "some." In common conversation, we tend to contrast "some" with "others." That is, to say that *some* Christians are followers of Jesus Christ implies (we think) that other Christians are *not* followers of Jesus Christ. But in logic, when we say that some *S* are *P*, we are saying *nothing* about whether other *S* are *P*.

Notice that, if two statements are related by implication, then they are also necessarily consistent.

3. **Logical equivalence:** If two statements are logically equivalent, then the first must imply the second, and the second must imply the first. If they are logically equivalent, then both statements must be true, or they must both be false. It is not possible for one to be true and the other false. For an example, we may look at:

P: *No Christians are Buddhists.*

Q: *No Buddhists are Christians.*

If *P* is true, then *Q* must also be true. And if *Q* is true, then *P* must be true. They both imply the other. In this case, they are both true. If we substituted the word *Americans* for *Buddhists*, then both statements would have been false. It is *false* that no Americans are Buddhists, and it must also be false that no Buddhists are Americans.

Similarly, these two statements are logically equivalent:

P: *Some mammals are egg-layers.*

Q: *Some egg-layers are mammals.*

Statements either of the form *No S is P* or of the form *Some S is P* are equivalent to the statements produced when the subject and predicate of each are reversed. We will consider these and other types of equivalent statements in more detail later.

4. **Independence:** If the truth or falsity of one statement has nothing at all to do with the truth or falsity of the other, we say they are independent.

There are two indications we may use to help determine if statements are independent. The relationship of independence can be determined by looking

**14**

at two other relationships. First, neither statement can imply the other, and second, the statements must be consistent.

In other words, neither statement can necessitate the truth of the other statement (implication), and neither statement can necessitate the falsity of the other (inconsistency).

Here are two statements which are independent.

*All Christians have had their sins forgiven.*

*All tricycles have three wheels.*

If one statement implies another, then the two are not independent. If one statement contradicts another, then the two are not independent. In this case, neither statement implies the other, and neither statement conflicts with the other.

These relationships can be organized as shown:

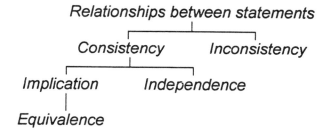

**Summary:** Four basic relationships between statements are *consistency, implication, logical equivalence,* and *independence.* Any two statements can be examined in order to determine whether these relationships apply.

## Exercise Four

With the following five sets of statements, circle **Y** if the statements are consistent, circle **N** if they are not consistent.

1.  *The sun is hot.*
    *The moon is white.*         Y     N

2.  *Paul was the author of Romans.*
    *Peter was the author of Romans.*     Y     N

3.  *Sally told a lie once.*
    *Sally usually tells the truth.*     Y     N

4.  *All fish have fins.*
    *Some fish do not have fins.*     Y     N

5.  *God knows all things.*
    *God does not know all things.*     Y     N

With the next five sets of statements, circle **Y** if the first sentence implies the second, circle **N** if it does not.

6.  *God created everything.*
    *God created porcupines.*     Y     N

7.  *All watermelons are green.*
    *Some watermelons are green.*     Y     N

8.  *Honey is sweet.*
    *I hate honey.*     Y     N

9.  *The Bible is the Word of God.*
    *Ecclesiastes is the Word of God.*     Y     N

10.  *Some trees are tall.*
    *All trees are tall.*     Y     N

Now seek to determine whether the statements in these sets are logically equivalent. If they are equivalent, circle Y, if not circle N.

11. *No Baptists are Americans.*
    *No Americans are Baptists.*                    **Y    N**

12. *All dogs are four-legged animals.*
    *All four-legged animals are dogs.*             **Y    N**

13. *No apples are oranges.*
    *No oranges are bananas.*                       **Y    N**

14. *Some apostles were Scripture-writers.*
    *Some Scripture-writers were apostles.*         **Y    N**

15. *No watermelons are cherries.*
    *No cherries are watermelons.*                  **Y    N**

Lastly, examine these sets to determine independency. Circle Y if the statements are independent, circle N if they are not independent.

16. *The typewriter is broken.*
    *Obadiah is my favorite book.*                  **Y    N**

17. *Logic is hard.*
    *Spanish is hard.*                              **Y    N**

18. *God created all the stars.*
    *God created this star.*                        **Y    N**

19. *Some triangles are yellow.*
    *Some tricycles are red.*                       **Y    N**

20. *Alan wrote this poem..*
    *Alan wrote all poems.*                         **Y    N**

## Consistency and Disagreement

Sometimes the consistency of statements is difficult to determine. Two statements may appear to be inconsistent, but upon close examination they turn out to be consistent. When there appears to be inconsistency, we have a *disagreement*. There are three kinds of disagreements that concern us here.

1. **Real disagreements**: This is true inconsistency. Both statements cannot be true at the same time. For example:

*Jesus is the Son of God.*

*Jesus is not the Son of God.*

Between these two statements there is real disagreement. Both cannot be true at the same time.

2. **Apparent disagreement**: Apparent disagreements are frequently the result of differences of opinion or perception. For example:

Smith: *I think Logic is easy.*

Jones: *I think Logic is the hardest course I have ever taken.*

Of course there is no true disagreement here. Both statements are self-reports, and both can therefore be taken as true without contradiction. There is a difference of opinion, but there is no logical contradiction.

Similarly, two people can disagree over the color of a particular object without really contradicting each other. I might think my shirt is blue, while you call it green. This is simply a difference in perception, and is thus an apparent disagreement.

3. **Verbal disagreement**: When different definitions are used for the same words, verbal disagreements can result. This does not necessarily mean that there is true inconsistency. For example:

Murphy: *One fifth of all high school graduates are illiterate.*

Johnson: *One third of all high school graduates are illiterate.*

This difference between Murphy and Johnson certainly looks like an inconsistency. But the key question here concerns the possible definitions of the word *illiterate*. Suppose Murphy intends the word to mean those who cannot read at all, and Johnson means those who cannot read past a second grade level. If they are not careful, they might find themselves in a forty-five minute debate before realizing that they don't really disagree.

Because of the possibility of verbal disagreements, it is extremely important *to define terms* in the first part of any debate. Consider the following question: "If a tree falls down in the forest, and nobody hears it, does it make a sound?" Some would say yes, and others would say no. But their disagreement would almost certainly be based upon how they are defining the word *sound*.

**Summary:** We have considered three common types of disagreements. Real disagreements are a true inconsistency between the statements. Apparent disagreements are differences in opinion or perception. Verbal disagreements result from differences in definition.

Give examples of the three types of disagreements.

## Real disagreement

1. Luther: _____

   Erasmus: _____

2. Lee: _____

   Grant: _____

## Apparent disagreement

3. Peter: _____

   Paul: _____

4. Homer: _____

   Virgil: _____

## Verbal disagreement (underline the word being defined differently)

5. William: _____

   Robert: _____

6. Write two statements which are consistent but not independent.

   _____

   _____

## The One Basic Verb

With the approach we are taking in this text, there is only one verb that needs to be mastered. This is the verb of being — that is, *is, are, was, were, will be*, and so on. Although it may seem awkward at first, this is done to help us analyze statements in arguments. Instead of saying *No cows eat meat*, we would change the verb and say *No cows are meat-eaters*. Another example:

*John runs swiftly.*

*John is a swift runner.*

As statements are placed into arguments, it is helpful to avoid the verbs of ordinary conversation. As mentioned, this makes analysis of the argument simpler. It does not mean, however, that there are no pitfalls. Even the word *is* can carry different definitions. Consider the following:

*God is love.*

*Love is blind.*

*Ray Charles is blind.*

Therefore *Ray Charles is God.*

There is obviously a problem here. But where is it? The argument is fallacious because it treats each usage of the word *is* as though it were an equal sign (A = B, B = C, D = C, therefore D = A). But *is* does not always have this meaning, as we see here. Again, make sure of your definitions.

Two more examples of verb translation should suffice. In doing the translations from ordinary verbs, remember that the purpose is not to enable you to write gripping prose, but rather to help analyze statements carefully in arguments.

*Henry throws rocks.*

*Henry is a rock-thrower.*

*Paul rebuked Peter at Antioch.*

*Paul was a Peter-at-Antioch rebuker.*

And now we go right into practical application. "*The logic student works on Exercise Six*" would become...?

**Summary:** In order to help us analyze statements, they must be translated so that they only use the verb of being (*is, are, was, were,* etc.)

## Exercise Six

In the blank below each sentence, rewrite the sentence using only the verb of being.

1. *John eats turnips.*

_____

2. *Rebekah reads her Bible daily.*

_____

3. *Paul resisted Peter and Barnabas.*

_____

4. *Susan works hard to resist temptation.*

_____

5. *Faith produces fruit.*

_____

6. *The works of the sinful nature lead to death.*

_____

7. *The donkey rebuked the prophet.*

_____

8. *The man will sing loudly.*

_____

9. *Absalom rebelled against King David.*

_____

10. *God created heaven and earth.*

_____

*Introductory Logic*

## Standard Categorical Statements

Categorical statements are statements which affirm or deny something about a given subject. Every categorical statement can be translated into one of four forms. The forms are as follows:

1. All *S* are *P*.
2. No *S* are *P*.
3. Some *S* are *P*.
4. Some *S* are not *P*.

Now how can a statement be translated into one of these forms? Let us take a sentence that could occur in everyday conversation.

*Nobody shuts the door.*

First we change the verb and the sentence becomes...

*Nobody is a door-shutter.*

Then the sentence can be put into one of our four forms.

*No person is a door-shutter.*

Each statement has quantity and quality. The quantity identifies whether the statement is universal (*all* and *no*) or particular (*some* and *some...not*). The quality identifies whether the statement is affirmative (*all* and *some*), or negative (*no* and *some...not*). There are four combinations of quantity and quality, which give us our four standard categorical statements:

| Statement | Quantity | Quality |
|---|---|---|
| All *S* are *P* | *Universal* | *Affirmative* |
| No *S* are *P* | *Universal* | *Negative* |
| Some *S* are *P* | *Particular* | *Affirmative* |
| Some *S* are not *P* | *Particular* | *Negative* |

Statements have two parts — a subject and a predicate. The subject is usually symbolized by the letter *S*, and the predicate is symbolized by the letter *P*. In a categorical statement, a relationship is expressed between two classes of objects, the subject class and the predicate class, i.e. people on the one hand

and door-shutters on the other.

In developing a formal argument, the statements must be put into a standard form. The rules for categorical statements are as follows:

1. The statements must begin with the words *all, no* or *some.*

2. The verb must be the verb of being: *is, are, was, were, will be,* etc.

3. Both the subject and the predicate must be a noun or a noun clause.

We have already covered the first two rules. The third is not at all difficult to understand. For example, we do not say...

*All dogs are brown.*

The proper form would be as follows:

*All dogs are brown animals.*

This is because *brown* is a mere adjective, whereas *brown animals* gives us the noun we need. Another example should suffice.

*Some houses are big.*

*Some houses are big structures.*

Then, to better understand and analyze our arguments, abbreviations are used for the sake of convenience. Consequently, the above statement changes to:

Some *H* are *B.*

**Summary:** There are four types of categorical statements: universal affirmative, universal negative, particular affirmative, and particular negative. These may be translated into standard categorical form: *All S is P, No S is P, Some S is P, Some S is not P,* respectively. In each of these, a relationship is expressed between the subject *S* and the predicate *P.*

## Exercise Seven

In the following exercise, analyze each statement. In the blank at the right, put down what sort of categorical statement it is, i.e. universal affirmative, universal negative, particular affirmative, or particular negative.

1. *Some cowboys are intellectuals.* _____

2. *All Scripture is God-breathed writing.* _____

3. *Some Christians are not students.* _____

4. *No Christians are Hindus.* _____

5. *Some books are pornography.* _____

6. *Some writers are not Christians.* _____

7. *All dogs are carnivores.* _____

8. *No cats are musicians.* _____

9. *Some soldiers are not brave men.* _____

10. *All men are mortal.* _____

With the next sentences, translate them in one of the four forms.

11. *Christians are not condemned.*

_____

12. *Every false teacher attacks the authority of Scripture.*

_____

13. *A few churches allow divorce too easily.*

_____

14. *Many people do not believe in the devil.*

_____

## The Square of Opposition

    We have already considered some relationships between statements. Now that we have a grasp of the four categorical statement forms, we will consider some new relationships. These relationships result from comparing statements in a special arrangement called the square of opposition.

    Universal affirmative statements are also called **A** statements. Below is the translation of an **A** statement.

    1. *Everyone who goes to our church believes in God.*

    2. *All our church-goers believe in God.*

    3. *All our church-goers are God-believers.*

    4. *All C are G.*

    Universal negative statements are also known as **E** statements. Notice below the transformation of an **E** statement.

    1. *None of my friends understand Algebra.*

    2. *No friends of mine understand Algebra.*

    3. *No friends of mine are Algebra-understanders.*

    4. *No F are A.*

    Particular affirmative statements can be referred to as **I** statements, and are translated as so:

    1. *Many Christians know a lot about the Bible.*

    2. *Some Christians know a lot about the Bible.*

    3. *Some Christians are Bible-knowers.*

    4. *Some C are B.*

And finally, particular negative statements are also known as **O** statements. They can be changed in this fashion.

1. *Many books in the Bible do not have a reference to Satan in them.*

2. *Some books in the Bible do not have a reference to Satan in them.*

3. *Some Bible books are not Satan-referencers.*

4. *Some B are not S.*

Now the four types of categorical statements are related to one another (provided they contain the same subject and predicate). There is a simple way to diagram the various relationships which is called the **square of opposition**.

The square of opposition demonstrates how **A**, **E**, **I** and **O** statements are related. Each one of the statements are located at a different corner of the square. The universals are placed at the top and the particulars at the bottom. The affirmatives are on the left and the negatives on the right. It looks like this:

| | |
|---|---|
| All S are P | No S are P |
| | |
| Some S are P | Some S are not P |

If we substitute our abbreviations for the categorical statements, it then looks like this:

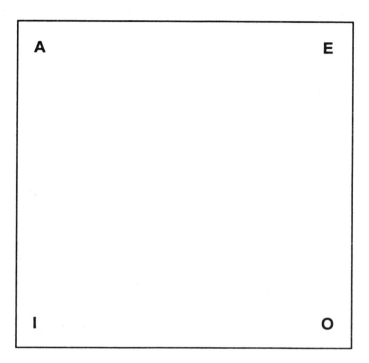

**Summary:** The four categorical statements can be abbreviated using the letters **A**, **E**, **I** and **O**. These can be placed into the corners of the square of opposition, which will allow us to analyze the relationships between the statements.

## Contradiction

There are five different relationships between categorical statements. They are:

1. Contradiction
2. Contrariety
3. Subcontrariety
4. Subimplication
5. Superimplication

We will consider contradiction first. Contradiction is the relationship between **A** and **O** statements, and **I** and **E** statements. First look at **A** and **O**.

An **A** statement would be: *All S are P.*

An **O** statement would be: *Some S are not P.*

Between the two statements there is obvious contradiction. The contradiction remains obvious if we remove the abbreviations.

*All Christians are forgiven sinners.*

*Some Christians are not forgiven sinners.*

A contradiction also exists between **I** and **E** statements.

An **I** statement would be: *Some S are P.*

An **E** statement would be: *No S are P.*

Again, the situation is unchanged if we substitute terms for our S's and P's.

*Some Christians are forgiven drunkards.*

*No Christians are forgiven drunkards.*

In the square of opposition, contradiction is represented by the diagonal lines which are drawn from one corner to another. A line can be drawn from **A** to **O**, or from **I** to **E**. These lines, which form an X, represent contradiction.

This contradiction means that both statements cannot be true. It is also not possible for both to be false. If one statement is true, the other must be false, and vice versa.

This can be illustrated with the example given above. If it is *true* that some Christians are forgiven drunkards, then it must be *false* that none are. If it is *false* that some Christians are forgiven drunkards, then it must be *true* that none are.

This also means that contradictory statements do not have the relationship of consistency, which we discussed earlier. Consistent statements were statements which could both be true.


**Summary:** In the square of opposition, the statements in the opposite corner are contradictory statements. If one is true, the other one must be false. This relationship exists between **A** and **O** statements, and **I** and **E** statements.

## Exercise Eight

In the space provided, draw six squares of opposition. With the first one, at the appropriate corners, place the four categorical statements, using the abbreviations *S* and *P*. With the second square, place **A**, **E**, **I** or **O** at the appropriate corner. On the third square, enter the letters again, and draw in the appropriate lines of contradiction. On the fourth square, use *dogs* as the subject and *cats* as the predicate (so the upper left-hand corner of that square would say *All dogs are cats*).

In the last two squares, make up categorical statements of your own and place them in the appropriate corners.

## Exercise Nine

Analyze the following arguments. Each of them contain two contradictory statements. Isolate those statements (ignoring the extra), translate them into categorical statements with the same subject and predicate, and diagram where they are located on the square of opposition. Please show all your work.

1. All logic students can see the problem here. While it may be true that some of them cannot see the problem, they will if they think about it.

2. There is no good reason to believe that the Bible is the Word of God; it is simply the word of men. I admit that prophecies which were fulfilled is one good reason to believe it, though I am still unconvinced.

## Contrariety

A contrary relationship is that which exists between **A** and **E** statements. In this relationship, it is not possible for both statements to be true. It is possible, however, for both to be false. For example, here are two contrary statements.

*All astronauts are men.*

*No astronauts are men.*

These statements can be abbreviated:

*All A are M.*

*No A are M.*

It is not possible for both these statements to be true. If all astronauts are men, then it is false that none are. If none are men, then it is false that all are.

At the same time, it is possible for both to be false. Consider the fact that some space shuttle astronauts were women, and others were men. In such a situation, both statements are clearly false.

It is important to remember the distinction between contradiction and contrariety. Contradictory statements cannot both be true at the same time, and cannot both be false at the same time. With contrariety, both cannot be true simultaneously, but both *can* be false at the same time.

The relationship of contrariety is represented by the top horizontal line of the square of opposition. When the terms are the same, all **A** and **E** statements are contrary. Here is another example.

*All snakes are green.*

*No snakes are green.*

We would abbreviate these to:

*All S are G.*

*No S are G.*

You should be able to see that, while both of these statements may be false, they cannot both be true.

*Statements and Their Relationships*

We will now turn to an attempt to identify a contrary relationship in a discussion between two Christians who differ on the mode of baptism.

Jones argued vigorously, "I maintain that all the baptisms in the New Testament were by immersion." Smith was not at all daunted, and said, "And I maintain that nobody in the New Testament was baptized by immersion."

How should we understand this dispute? Is it a contradiction, or is it a clash of contrary statements? Let's break their assertions down.

Jones: *All the baptisms in the New Testament were by immersion.*

*All New Testament baptisms were immersions.*

*All B were I.*

Smith: *Nobody in the New Testament was baptized by immersion.*

*No New Testament baptisms were immersions.*

*No B were I.*

Now we can place both these statements on the square of opposition and see that the first is an **A** statement, and the second is an **E** statement. This means, necessarily, that both Smith and Jones cannot be correct. The two positions exclude one another. It is possible, however, for both to be wrong. What if the New Testament teaches that two modes of baptism are used? This is not an assertion that it does so, but rather a reminder that the *logical* possibility exists.

What would the situation be if Smith maintained that some baptisms were not immersions? His statement would then be *Some B are not I*.

This would be a relationship of contradiction. If *All B are I* is true, then *Some B are not I* is false. If *Some B are not I* is true, then *All B are I* is false. In this case, either Jones or Smith would have to be correct. Both could not be wrong.

It may seem initially that the clash of *all* and *no* is more fundamental that the clash of *all* and *some...not*. This is not the case. In a clash between *all* and *no*, both can share a claim to falsehood. But between *all* and *some...not*, one of them must be true.

Consider one more example. Sally is saying that all the girls in the high school are stuck up and proud (*All G are P*). Jane thinks that Sally is confused and that none of them are (*No G are P*).

But if it is true that only some of the girls are proud, then both Sally and Jane are wrong. Both cannot be right, but both can be wrong.

**Summary: A** and **E** statements have a relationship of contrariety. Both cannot be true, but both can be false. This should not be confused with the relationship of contradiction, where both cannot be true, and both cannot be false.

## Subcontrariety

Subcontrariety is the relationship which exists between **I** statements and **O** statements. It is represented by a horizontal line on the bottom of the square of opposition.

It is possible for both an **I** statement and an **O** statement to be true. But it is not possible for both to be false. The relationship of subcontrariety is the opposite of contrariety, as seen by lining them up:

**Contrariety:**      Both statements cannot be true, but they can both be false.

**Subcontrariety:**   Both statements can be true, but they cannot both be false.

For example, here are an **I** statement and an **O** statement respectively.

*Some preachers are boring speakers.*

*Some preachers are not boring speakers.*

Think about this for a moment. Is it possible for both of these statements to be true? Is the world big enough to contain preachers who are not boring, as well as those who are? Certainly. Pastor Jones, for example, may be as boring as they come, while Pastor Smith is not at all boring.

But is it possible for both statements to be false at the same time? *No, it is not.*

Think for a moment. If it is *false* that some preachers are boring, this is the same thing as saying that no preachers are boring. And if no preachers are boring, then certainly some preachers are not boring — because all preachers are not boring.

Consider another example:

*Some students are intelligent.*

*Some students are not intelligent.*

To see that both of these can be true is not that difficult. There will perhaps be more difficulty in understanding why both cannot be false.

If it is *false* that some students are not intelligent, that is the same as saying that all students are intelligent (by contradiction). If all students are intelligent, then it must be true that some students are intelligent (by implication). And if it is *true* that some students are intelligent, then it cannot be *false* that some are (by the laws of thought). Thus they cannot both be false.

**Summary:** On the square of opposition, the two particular statements are related by subcontrariety. I statements are subcontrary to O statements, and O statements are subcontrary to I statements. The relationship of subcontrariety means that both statements can be true, but they cannot both be false.

## Exercise Ten

Analyze the following paragraphs, isolate the related statements, and put them into categorical form. Assign abbreviations to the terms, and place them on the square of opposition. One will show the relationship of contradiction, one the relationship of contrariety, and one subcontrariety. Show your work.

1.  Johnny sneered at Billy, "All third-graders are stupid!" Billy shouted back, ineffectively countering Johnny's point, "That's not true! None of them are!"

2. Smith said, "Pro-lifers don't care about children who are already born. All they care about is their stupid political agenda." Jones disagreed, "No, there are many pro-lifers who are involved in helping children."

3.  Some people I know are always complaining about their jobs; they never seem to quit. Of course, not everyone complains.

## Subimplication

In the relationship of **subimplication**, the truth of a particular statement can be inferred from the truth of its corresponding universal. Given the truth of a universal **A** statement, the truth of the corresponding particular statement (in this case, an **I** statement) is implied. The same can be said of the other universal/particular relationship (which is **E** to **O**).

If an **A** statement is true, then its corresponding **I** statement must be true. If an **E** statement is true, then its corresponding **O** statement must be true.

What follows is an example of subimplication.

**A** statement: *All Christians are loved by God.*

**I** statement: *Some Christians are loved by God.*

If it true that all Christians are loved by God, then it must be true that some of them are. It cannot be false that some Christians are loved by God if all of them are.

Here is an example of subimplication between an **E** and **O**.

**E** statement: *No logicians are blonds.*

**O** statement: *Some logicians are not blonds.*

If it is true that no logicians are blonds, then it must be true that some are not blonds. It is not possible for this **O** statement to be false. If the **E** statement is true, then the **O** statement must also be true.

With subimplication, it is only possible to infer particular statements from universal statements. At the same time, if the universal *affirmative* statement is being used, then the inference is only possible with the particular *affirmative* statement. For example, subimplication goes from **A** to **I**, and from **E** to **O**. It does *not* go from **A** to **O**, or **E** to **I** (which, of course, is contradiction).

On the square of opposition, the relationship of subimplication can be pictured with two arrows on either side of the square, going from top to bottom.

The relationship of subimplication has nothing to do with *falsity*. It is concerned solely with the implication of truth. The truth of particular statements is inferred from the truth of the corresponding universal statement.

Thus we see that the examples of implication given earlier in the text were actually more specifically examples of *sub*implication.

**Summary:** Subimplication is the relationship from **A** to **I** statements, and **E** to **O** statements. In this relationship, the truth of the universal affirmative implies the truth of the particular affirmative. In the same way, the truth of the universal negative implies the truth of the particular negative.

### Superimplication

As we have learned, subimplication is the implication of truth for one statement on the basis of the truth of another. In contrast to this, **superimplication** is the implication of falsity.

With subimplication, the inference is from a universal statement to a particular statement (**A** to **I**, or **E** to **O**). This relationship was pictured by vertical arrows on either side of the square of opposition, going from top to bottom.

In the relationship of superimplication, the arrows go up the other way (from **I** to **A**, or **O** to **E**).

In superimplication, given the falsity of a particular statement, the falsity of its corresponding universal is implied. In other words, the falsity of an **A** statement can be inferred from the falsity of an **I** statement. In the same way, the falsity of an **E** statement can be inferred from the falsity of an **O** statement. For example:

**I** statement: *Some Christians are atheists.*

**A** statement: *All Christians are atheists.*

This is straightforward. If it is false that some Christians are atheists, then it must be false that all of them are. Understanding the relationship between **O** and **E** statements is perhaps a little more difficult.

**O** statement: *Some test answers are not correct.*

**E** statement: *No test answers are correct.*

Work through this carefully. If it is *false* that some test answers are not correct, then it must be false that no test answers are correct. In other words, if it is false that some test answers are not correct, then it must be true that all of them are correct (by contradiction). If all of them were correct, then it must be false that none were correct (by contrariety).

Remember that between **A** and **I** statements, and **E** and **O** statements, there are *two* relationships — subimplication and superimplication. With the relationships previously studied, the arrow between the letters should be understood as a two-way street. **A** to **O** and **O** to **A** have the same relationship — contradiction. But with subimplication and superimplication, the arrow goes only one way.

We can now draw the complete square of opposition, including all of the relationship lines.

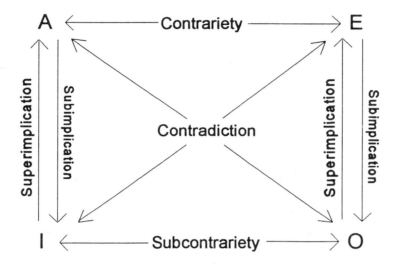

**Summary:** A relationship of superimplication exists from **I** to **A** statements, and from **O** to **E** statements. In this relationship, if the particular statement is false, then its corresponding universal statement is false. This completes the relationships on the square of opposition.

**Exercise Eleven**

In the following exercise, write the relationship which exists between the two given statements in the blank at right. Their order does matter.

1. *All cowboys are rough men.*
   *Some cowboys are not rough men.*                    _____

2. *Some ladies are not rude women.*
   *No ladies are rude women.*                          _____

3. *All Christians are forgiven sinners.*
   *Some Christians are forgiven sinners.*              _____

4. *No Christians are Muslims.*
   *Some Christians are not Muslims.*                   _____

5. *All french fries are greasy food.*
   *No french fries are greasy food.*                   _____

6. *Some pictures are beautiful art.*
   *Some pictures are not beautiful art.*               _____

7. *Some atheists are irrational men.*
   *No atheists are irrational men.*                    _____

8. *All eighth graders are brilliant logicians.*
   *Some eighth graders are brilliant logicians.*       _____

9. *All violinists are right-handed players.*
   *Some violinists are not right-handed players.*      _____

10. *Some feminists are feminine.*
    *All feminists are feminine.*                       _____

11. *All Democrats are Republicans.*
    *Some Democrats are not Republicans.*               _____

12. *All conservatives are reactionaries.*
    *Some conservatives are reactionaries.*             _____

*Statements and Their Relationships*

## Exercise Twelve

1. Draw the square of opposition, including all the arrows and relationships. Include the abbreviated categorical statements in the corners, using *S* and *P*.

Identify the relationships between statements described.

2. One must be true and the other must be false.　　　_____

3. Both can be true, but both cannot be false.　　　_____

4. If the particular is false, its universal is false.　　　_____

Write a set of statements which are related by

5. Contrariety　_____

　　　_____

6. Contradiction_____

　　　_____

7. Subimplication_____

　　　_____

In the following problems, assume that the first statement in each set is true. Then determine the truth value of each remaining statement in the set. Circle **T** if it is true, **F** if it is false, and **?** If the truth value cannot be determined.

8. All students are young people.

    No students are young people.      T    F    ?

    Some students are young people.      T    F    ?

9. No angels are demons.

    Some angels are demons.      T    F    ?

    Some angels are not demons.      T    F    ?

10. Some computers are word processors.

    All computers are word processors.      T    F    ?

    No computers are word processors.      T    F    ?

11. Some laws are not biblical laws.

    All laws are biblical laws.      T    F    ?

    No laws are biblical laws.      T    F    ?

Translate the following statements into standard categorical form. Do not abbreviate.

12. Students never eat frog legs.

_____

13. Many children make mud pies.

_____

14. Everybody has sinned.

_____

15. A few of the problems were not hard.

_____

# SYLLOGISMS AND VALIDITY

## Arguments

Many people think an argument is nothing more than a quarrelsome disagreement. But as the word is used in logic, it means nothing of the kind. A quarrel occurs when people are irritated or angry with each other. In formal logic, an **argument** is simply a set of statements, one of which appears to be implied or supported by the others.

There are two types of statements in an argument. The first type is called a **premise**. The second is called a **conclusion**. The conclusion is the point or terminus of the argument, the statement which appears to be implied or supported by the others. The premises are those statements which support or imply the conclusion.

An argument will never contain more than one conclusion. It can contain more than one premise. When you hear words like *therefore, thus, so,* and *consequently,* there is reason to believe that you are about to hear the conclusion of an argument. Words which indicate premises are *since, because, for,* and *given that.* If a statement in an argument is immediately followed by words indicating a premise, it is probably the conclusion. This statement you are now reading must be a conclusion, because it is followed by the word *because.*

The following is an example of a formal argument, written in informal language.

*The Bible is the Word of God, and the book of Jonah is definitely in the Bible. We must therefore conclude that the book of Jonah is the Word of God.*

There are two premises here. The first is that the Bible is the Word of God. The second is that the book of Jonah is in the Bible. The conclusion, which follows from this, is that the book of Jonah is the Word of God.

Here is an argument which is similar in form, but in which the conclusion does *not* follow from the premises.

*The Bible is the Word of God, and the Book of Mormon is definitely not in the Bible. We must therefore conclude that the Book of Mormon is not the Word of God.*

Christians must take special care in situations like this. Just because you agree with the conclusion (that the Book of Mormon is not the Word of God) does *not* mean the argument is a good one. The question is *not* whether the conclusion is true, *but whether it follows from the premises.* In this case it does not. The premises contain no information about whether the Bible is the *only* word from God. If the premise had said that the Bible was the sole Word of God, then the conclusion would have been warranted. Look at a similar argument where the error is a little more obvious.

*Given that the letter is from Miss Jones, and that this message is definitely not in the letter, we must therefore conclude that Miss Jones did not write this message.*

The problem should be obvious. The premises don't tell us that the letter was the only thing that Miss Jones ever wrote.

**Summary:** An argument is a set of statements, one of which (the conclusion) appears to be implied by the others (the premises). Arguments contain only one conclusion, which usually starts with *therefore, thus, so,* or *in conclusion.* Arguments may contain more than one premise. Premises usually start with *because, since, for* or *given that.* In a good argument, the conclusion is supported or implied by the premises.

## Exercise 13

Underline the conclusion in each of the following arguments.

1. All theology is a study in infinity, so all calculus problems are theology, because all calculus problems are a study in infinity.

2. All space stations are important research, but some space stations are not a product of American ingenuity. Therefore some important research is not a product of American ingenuity.

3. Some pagans are idolaters, because no pagans are Christians, and no Christians are idolators.

4. All objects in free fall are weightless, and all meteors are objects in free fall. Therefore all meteors are weightless.

5. All marsupials are pouched animals, and some marsupials are not Australian mammals. Consequently, some Australian mammals are not pouched animals.

6. Some Socratic sages are not perspicacious people, since some Socratic sages are metaphorical masters, and some perspicacious people are also metaphorical masters.

7. All murderers are criminals, and some heroes of the faith were murderers, from which it follows that some criminals are heroes of the faith.

8. No street legal vehicles are stock cars. Thus no racing car is street legal, since all stock cars are racing cars.

9. Some conclusions are not easily located statements, for all easily located statements are sentences at the end of arguments, and some sentences at the end of arguments are not conclusions.

10. Given that some pagan literature is great writing, and no great writing is worthless instructional material, we must conclude that some pagan literature is not worthless instructional material.

## Truth and Validity

When the student of logic examines an argument, the first thing he should look for is **validity**. We say that an argument is valid if the conclusion is necessarily true given that the premises are true. In other words, if the premises are true, and the argument is valid, then the conclusion *has* to be true. If an argument has true premises and a false conclusion, we know it is invalid.

In a valid argument, the premises may be false. But *if* they were true, the conclusion would have to be true also. Here is an example of a valid argument. One of the premises happens to be false, but the argument remains valid.

*Given the fact that all dogs are brown, and that all poodles are dogs, it follows necessarily that all poodles are brown.*

If it were in fact true that all dogs were brown, then all poodles would *necessarily* be brown. The problem with the argument is the falsehood of the first premise, not the structure of the argument. To test for validity, grant provisional "truth" to the premises, and then see if the conclusion would have to be true.

Here is an example of an invalid argument, with all true premises, and a true conclusion.

*Given the fact that all dogs are mammals, and that all dogs are canines, it follows necessarily that all canines are mammals.*

Both of the above premises are true, and the conclusion is also true. But, if you examine it carefully, you will see that the conclusion is not implied by the premises (substituting the word *animals* for *canines* makes this clear). It is this lack of implication which makes the argument invalid.

Once an argument has been examined for validity (and it is found to be valid), the argument may then be examined with a view toward the truth or falsehood of the conclusion. If the argument is invalid, then there is no reason to proceed further. But if it is found to be valid, it is still necessary to examine the truth of the premises. If they are found to be true, then the conclusion must be true as well.

If an argument is valid and the premises are true, it is called a **sound** argument. You should realize, then, that the conclusion of a sound argument must be true.

## Syllogisms and Validity

Do not confuse truth with validity! Once we learn the basic rules of formal logic, it is easy to see how prevalent this confusion is. In public debate, the applause is frequently reserved, not for those who reason well, but for those with whom the audience agrees. Unfortunately, this is a common problem in the church.

Here is a final example where the premises are true, and the conclusion is necessarily true.

*Given the fact that all Christians are forgiven, and that the apostle Paul was a Christian, it follows that the apostle Paul was forgiven.*

In this argument, the premises are true, the argument is valid, so the conclusion is *therefore* true. This is a sound argument.

The different types of arguments related to validity and truth can thus be arranged as shown.

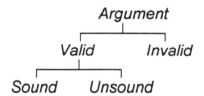

You can see from the chart that there are two ways for an argument to be bad. First, it can simply be invalid. Second, it can be valid, but unsound.

**Summary:** An argument is valid if the truth of the conclusion follows from the truth of the premises. If an argument has true premises and a false conclusion, it is invalid. The validity of an argument is not the same thing as the truth of the conclusion. An argument may be valid, with a false conclusion. It may be invalid, with a true conclusion. Or, as in a sound argument, it may be valid, and have a true conclusion.

## Exercise 14

In the last section, you saw examples of valid arguments with a false premise and a true conclusion, and true premises with a true conclusion. You also saw an invalid argument with true premises and a true conclusion. In this exercise, write arguments with the given criteria.

1. Valid argument, two false premises, false conclusion:

_____

_____

_____

2. Valid argument, two false premises, true conclusion:

_____

_____

_____

3. Invalid argument, two false premises, false conclusion:

_____

_____

_____

4. Invalid argument, two false premises, true conclusion:

_____

_____

_____

5. Invalid argument, two true premises, false conclusion:

_____

_____

_____

## The Syllogism

The syllogism is a particular form for organizing categorical statements into an argument. A categorical syllogism is made up of three categorical statements. The first two statements are the premises, and the last is the conclusion.

What follows is an example of a syllogism.

*All red plants are living things.*
*All roses are red plants.*
*Therefore, all roses are living things.*

If we abbreviate, our syllogism looks like this (the symbol ∴ means *therefore*).

*All M are P*
*All S are M*
*∴ All S are P*

All syllogisms contain three **terms**. The terms in the above syllogism are *S, P* and *M*. In order to structure an argument properly, it is necessary to have a good understanding of terms. The terms are called, respectively, the minor term, the major term and the middle term.

The **minor term** is the subject term of the conclusion. The minor term above was *roses*, or *S*.

The **major term** is the predicate term of the conclusion. In our syllogism, the major term was *living things*, or *P*.

The **middle term** is the term which is in both premises but which is not in the conclusion at all. It is called the middle term because it connects the premises together. In our example, the middle term was *red plants*, or *M*.

As you might suspect, the **major premise** is the premise which contains the major term. Traditionally, the major premise is the first premise in the argument. The **minor premise** is the premise which contains the minor term. There is no middle premise, only a middle term.

In our example above, the major premise was *All red plants are living things* (it contains the major term — living things). The minor premise was *All roses are red plants* (it contains the minor term — roses).

The conclusion follows because the argument is valid. If the premises were true, the conclusion would necessarily have to be true. (Note that the minor premise happens to be false, but this does not affect the validity of the syllogism.)

Consider the following syllogism:

*All ringed planets are gas giants, so no inner planets are ringed planets, since no inner planets are gas giants.*

This syllogism is not in the traditional order for standard categorical syllogisms. To put it into standard form, this procedure should be followed:

1. *Find the conclusion.*
   In our example, the conclusion is "No inner planets are ringed planets." We know this because it starts with the word *so* and precedes the word *since*.

2. *Find the major term.*
   The major term is the predicate of the conclusion. The major term of the example is *ringed planets.*

3. *Find the major premise.*
   The major premise is the premise containing the major term. Since the major term is *ringed planets*, the major premise is "All ringed planets are gas giants."

4. *Find the minor premise.*
   The minor premise contains the minor term. Obviously, it is also the statement which is neither the major premise nor the conclusion. In the example above, the minor premise is "No inner planets are gas giants." To check, we see that this does contain the minor term, *inner planets.*

5. *Write the syllogism out in standard order.*
   Standard order is: major premise, minor premise, conclusion. Thus the example syllogism in standard order is

   *All ringed planets are gas giants.*
   *No inner planets are gas giants.*
   *Therefore, no inner planets are ringed planets.*

**Summary:** A syllogism is an argument with one conclusion, two premises, and three terms. The minor term is the subject of the conclusion, the major term is the predicate of the conclusion, the middle term is not in the conclusion, but it is in both premises. The major premise is the premise containing the major term. The minor premise is the premise containing the minor term. The standard order for categorical syllogisms is: major premise, minor premise, conclusion.

## Exercise 15

Identify the major, minor and middle terms for each syllogism. The syllogisms are not necessarily in standard order.

1. All theology is a study in infinity, so all calculus problems are theology, because all calculus problems are a study in infinity.

*Major:*                    *Minor:*                    *Middle:*

2. All space stations are important research, but some space stations are not a product of American ingenuity. Therefore some important research is not a product of American ingenuity.

*Major:*                    *Minor:*                    *Middle:*

3. Some pagans are idolaters, because no pagans are Christians, and no Christians are idolators.

*Major:*                    *Minor:*                    *Middle:*

4. All objects in free fall are weightless, and all meteors are objects in free fall. Therefore all meteors are weightless.

*Major:*                    *Minor:*                    *Middle:*

5. All marsupials are pouched animals, and some marsupials are not Australian mammals. Consequently, some Australian mammals are not pouched animals.

*Major:*                    *Minor:*                    *Middle:*

Rewrite into standard order for categorical syllogisms:

6. Some Socratic sages are not perspicacious people, since some Socratic sages are metaphorical masters, and some perspicacious people are also metaphorical masters.

7. All murderers are criminals, and some heroes of the faith were murderers, from which it follows that some criminals are heroes of the faith.

8. No street legal vehicles are stock cars. Thus no racing car is street legal, since all stock cars are racing cars.

9. Some conclusions are not easily located statements, for all easily located statements are sentences at the end of arguments, and some sentences at the end of arguments are not conclusions.

10. Given that some pagan literature is great writing, and no great writing is worthless instructional material, we must conclude that some pagan literature is not worthless instructional material.

## Mood of Syllogisms

Because the syllogism is composed of categorical statements, the syllogism can be abbreviated following the same rules concerning the substitution of letters for terms. In this book, we will have a standard substitution for the various terms. **S** will represent the minor term, **P** will represent the major term, and **M** will represent the middle term.

Notice how the following syllogism is transformed.

*Some black cars are fast cars.*
*All Model T cars are black cars.*
*Therefore, some Model T cars are fast cars.*

This syllogism is invalid; the conclusion does not follow from the premises. Nevertheless, we may still abbreviate it in order to analyze it readily. When abbreviated, it looks like this:

*Some M are P*
*All S are M*
∴ *Some S are P*

When a syllogism is arranged in standard order, with the standard abbreviations for the terms, we call this arrangement a **schema**. If two arguments follow the same logical form, we can say that they have the same schema. For example, an argument which substituted *dogs* for *Model T cars*, *brown animals* for *black cars*, and *slow animals* for *fast cars*, would have the same schema as the argument above. In other words, the abbreviations for the two arguments would be identical.

We now come to what is called the **mood** of the syllogism. The mood refers to the various possible combinations of **A**, **E**, **I** and **O** statements which make up the syllogism. It tells you what kinds of statements the syllogism contains, and what order they come in. The mood of our syllogism above is **IAI**, because the major premise is an **I** statement, *Some M are P,* the minor premise is an **A** statement, *All S are M*, and the conclusion is an **I** statement, *Some S are P*. The mood is always given in standard order.

**Summary:** Terms in a syllogism may be abbreviated in just the same way they are in a categorical statement: *P* is the major term, *S* is the minor term, *M* is the middle term. A schema represents the structure of the syllogism. The mood of a syllogism shows the nature of the various statements in standard order.

## Figure of Syllogisms

The **figure** of a syllogism is a number identifying the placement of the middle term in the argument. There are four possible ways the middle term can be arranged in the two premises.

In figure 1, the middle term is the subject of the major premise and the predicate of the minor premise. Figure 2 is when the middle term is the predicate of both premises. Figure 3 is when the middle term is the subject of both premises. In figure 4, the middle term is the predicate of the major premise and the subject of the minor premise. The four possible figures can thus be diagramed as shown:

| Figure 1 | Figure 2 | Figure 3 | Figure 4 |
|---|---|---|---|
| M | M | M | M |
| M | M | M | M |

Consider the following syllogism, and note how the middle term is arranged according to the pattern of figure 1.

*No Hindus are Christians.*
*Some Indians are Hindus.*
*Therefore, some Indians are not Christians.*

The middle term is *Hindu*, because it occurs in both premises but not in the conclusion. In the major premise, *Hindu* is the subject. In the minor premise it is the predicate. If you look again at figure 1, you will see that this is the pattern for the figure 1 syllogism.

Now we will schematize the syllogism (i.e. we will set out its schema).

*No M are P*
*Some S are M*
*∴ Some S are not P.*

The mood of this syllogism is **EIO**. That is, the major premise is an **E** statement, the minor premise is an **I** statement, and the conclusion is an **O** statement. As we have already pointed out, it is also a figure 1.

We can therefore describe the syllogism as an **EIO-1**.

When the mood and the figure of the syllogism are listed together this way, we are describing the **form** of the syllogism. The form is the mood plus the figure.

Below are examples of schemas having figures 2, 3 and 4, all with the same mood, **AEO**.

| Figure 2 | Figure 3 | Figure 4 |
|---|---|---|
| All P is M | All M is P | All P is M |
| No S is M | No M is S | No M is S |
| ∴ Some S is not P | ∴ Some S is not P | ∴ Some S is not P |

Given that there are four possible types of categorical statements for each premise and the conclusion, and four possible figures, there are 4 × 4 × 4 × 4 possible combinations of mood and figure, that is, 256 forms of syllogisms. These are all shown in the Appendix.

**Summary:** The figure of a syllogism is a number identifying the placement of the middle term in the premises. The middle term may be the subject or predicate of each premise. There are four possible combinations. When this figure is listed after the mood, it is a description of the syllogism's form.

## Exercise 16

Determine the form (mood and figure) of the following syllogisms and write it on the blank. The first two are in standard order, the next two are not.

1. All Bibles are books.
   Some periodicals are not books.
   Therefore some periodicals are not Bibles.          _____

2. Some speeches are sermons.
   No sermons are short events.
   Thus some short events are not speeches.             _____

3. Some blondes are geniuses,
   because all students are geniuses,
   and all blondes are students.                        _____

4. No fish are mammals,
   so no snakes are mammals,
   since no fish are snakes.                             _____

Now develop your own syllogisms to meet the requirements of the given form. Make sure your syllogisms are in standard order.

5. **AEE-1**     _____
                 _____
                 _____

6. **EAO-2**     _____
                 _____
                 _____

7. **AII-3**     _____
                 _____
                 _____

8. **OAO-4**     _____
                 _____
                 _____

## Testing Syllogisms by Counterexample

The validity of syllogism is determined *solely* by the form. Validity is not determined by the meanings of the individual statements. Certain forms are always valid, and the other forms are not.

There are many ways to test the validity of a syllogism. The two this text are concerned with are testing by counterexamples and by rules.

We will begin our testing of syllogisms with counterexamples. How can you test a syllogism by counterexample? This is accomplished through the substitution of terms. Suppose someone has presented an argument like this:

> *Some Christians are not critical thinkers.*
> *Some humanists are not critical thinkers.*
> *Therefore, some humanists are Christians.*

The syllogism in invalid. This can be shown by recalling the definition of validity. We said that an argument *with true premises and a false conclusion is necessarily invalid.* If we were to substitute terms in this syllogism such that the premises were obviously true and the conclusion obviously false, we would show the syllogism to be invalid.

For example, let us substitute *women, men, and lawyers* for *Christians, humanists and critical thinkers*. The syllogism would then look like this.

> *Some women are not lawyers.*
> *Some men are not lawyers.*
> *Therefore, some men are women.*

Both syllogisms have the same form (**OOI-2**), and are therefore both valid, or both invalid. The second has an obviously absurd conclusion, and both premises are true. Some women are not lawyers, and some men are not. If both premises are true (and they are), and the conclusion is obviously false, then the problem has to be with the form of the syllogism. That is, it is invalid.

Let's consider another example (and counterexample)

> *No man is immortal.*
> *Some angels are not men.*
> *Therefore, some angels are immortal.*

To test with a counterexample, we want to construct a syllogism with the same form (**EOI-1**). We could do this:

**61**

*No dogs are horses.*
*Some cats are not dogs.*
*Therefore, some cats are horses.*

It is much easier to see the problem with the second syllogism than with the first. Nevertheless, both have the same form, and stand or fall together. If the second is invalid, then so is the first — of necessity.

Note that if you were testing an argument for validity but were unable to develop a counterexample, there is one of two possibilities. Either the argument is valid, so no counterexample is possible, or you are not being creative enough. If you suspect an argument is invalid, but you have not been able to think of a counterexample, try starting with just a false conclusion. Invent major and minor terms that when substituted make the conclusion false. Then write these terms in the premises, leaving the middle term blank. To finish the counterexample, you simply need to find a middle term that makes both the premises true.

For example, suppose you wanted to write a counterexample for this argument:

*All Paul's writings are first-century compositions.*
*Some epistles are not Paul's writings.*
*Therefore some epistles are not first-century compositions.*

To write a counterexample, we start by making the conclusion false. If we substitute *students* for *epistles,* and *people* for *first-century compositions*, we get

*All _____ are people.*
*Some students are not _____.*
*Therefore some students are not people.*

The conclusion is false (since all students are people), so we simply need to find a middle term to make the premises true. Many terms would work, so we will leave it up to you to finish.

**Summary:** An invalid argument may be exposed through the use of a counterexample. A counterexample is a syllogism of the same form as the original argument, but with obviously true premises and an obviously false conclusion.

## Exercise 17

Test the following syllogisms by counterexample. If no counterexample is possible, write "valid."

1. *Some cherubim are not angels.*
   *Some angels are not seraphim.*
   *Therefore, all seraphim are cherubim.*

   _____

   _____

   _____

2. *No wind instruments are guitars.*
   *All wind instruments are expensive instruments.*
   *Therefore, no expensive instrument is a guitar.*

   _____

   _____

   _____

3. *All NIV Bibles are Zondervan publications.*
   *Some KJV Bibles are not Zondervan publications.*
   *Therefore, no KJV Bible is an NIV Bible.*

   _____

   _____

   _____

4. *Some Baptists are not Presbyterians.*
   *No Nazarene is a Baptist.*
   *Therefore, all Nazarenes are Presbyterians.*

_____

_____

_____


5. *All Calvinists are predestinarians.*
   *No predestinarian is an Arminian.*
   *Therefore, some Arminians are not Calvinists.*

_____

_____

_____


6. *Some colds are not fatal diseases.*
   *All cancers are fatal diseases.*
   *Therefore, some cancers are not colds.*

_____

_____

_____


**Challenge:** Work through the 256 forms of syllogisms in the Appendix, using counterexamples to find the invalid ones. There are 232 invalid forms, and 24 valid ones. As you work through them, remember that if you cannot figure out a counterexample, it is either valid, or you need to be more creative. Also, you would be greatly assisted in working through them more quickly if you recall what you learned about relationships between statements. Good luck!

## Distributed Terms

We have seen that counterexamples are one method for determining the invalidity of syllogisms. You may also have realized that the method of counterexamples is not very helpful when the syllogism happens to be valid. Because of this, we need another method for testing syllogisms for validity.

This method involves the use of rules. Because these rules depend upon an understanding of **distributed terms**, we will define them first. The terms in a syllogism are said to be either distributed or undistributed. By distributed term, we mean that the term refers to all members of its class. We can tell if a term is distributed or not simply by its placement in a categorical statement. We will look at each categorical statement in turn.

*All S are P* — Here *S* is distributed and *P* is undistributed.

The *S* refers to all of its class, the *P* does not. The statement *All dogs are mammals* says something about all members of the subject class, all dogs, but it does not refer to all members of its predicate class. It does not say anything about *all* mammals. It only says that *some* of them are dogs.

*No S are P* — Both *S* and *P* are distributed.

The *S* refers to all of its class, and so does the *P*. For example, the statement *No dogs are cats* makes a claim about all dogs (they are not cats) and about all cats (they are not dogs).

*Some S are P* — Both *S* and *P* are undistributed.

No claim is being made about every *S* or every *P*. It only says that *some* of the *S* are *P*, and that *some* of the *P* are *S*.

*Some S are not P* — *S* is undistributed and *P* is distributed.

Consider the **O** statement *Some astronauts are not men.* This statement says nothing about all astronauts. It only says that *some* of them are not men. However, it does make a claim about all men. This claim is that all men are not those astronauts being referred to in the subject (namely, female astronauts).

It may help you to remember that the subjects of universal statements and the predicates of negative statements are distributed.

The rules for testing a syllogism are explained in the next section. You will quickly see why it is necessary to understand what a distributed term is.

## Testing Syllogisms by Rules

There are five rules for testing the validity of syllogisms. If *any* of these rules are violated, then a syllogism is invalid. If the syllogism passes all five, then it is valid. The rules are:

1. In at least one premise, the middle term must be distributed.
2. If a term is distributed in the conclusion, it must also be distributed in its premise.
3. A valid syllogism cannot have two negative premises.
4. A valid syllogism cannot have a negative premise and an affirmative conclusion.
5. A valid syllogism cannot have two affirmative premises and a negative conclusion.

Compare the last three rules. You should see that, if a syllogism has a negative conclusion, one premise must be affirmative and the other negative. You should also realize from these that if a syllogism has an affirmative conclusion, it must have two affirmative premises.

These can be combined even more briefly by this "rule": The number of negative conclusions in a syllogism must equal the number of negative premises. If a syllogism has zero negative conclusions (i.e. an affirmative conclusion), it must have zero negative premises. If it has one negative conclusion, it must have exactly one negative premise.

We will now discuss each of the rules in more detail.

Rule 1. *In at least one premise, the middle term must be distributed.* This means that the middle term must be either the subject of an **A** statement, the subject or predicate of an **E** statement, or the predicate of an **O** statement. Below is a small paradigm for use in applying the first two rules.

|        | S   | P   |
|--------|-----|-----|
| **A:** | d   | -   |
| **E:** | d   | d   |
| **I:** | -   | -   |
| **O:** | -   | d   |

When you are examining a syllogism, the first rule is applied by looking at what types of statements the middle term is in. For example, consider the following syllogism:

*All men are mortals.*
*No mortals are angels.*
*Therefore, some angels are not men.*

When we consider our first rule, we see that the middle term is *mortals*. The middle term occurs in two types of statements, an **A** and an **E**. Now the middle term is not distributed in the **A** statement, because it is the predicate. It is distributed in the **E** statement, because both terms are distributed in an **E** statement. The syllogism therefore passes its first test.

When this rule is broken, it is known as the **Fallacy of the Undistributed Middle**. Here is an example in which this fallacy is made:

*All men are created beings.*
*Some created beings are angels.*
*Therefore, some angels are men.*

The middle term, *created beings,* is not distributed in either premise. Thus, this syllogism is invalid; it has an undistributed middle.

The reasoning behind this rule is as follows: The middle term connects the two premises. If the middle term is undistributed in both, meaning that in neither premise does it refer to all of its members, then no necessary connection is being made between the premises. In the example, the *created beings* of the major premise is a separate class from the *created beings* of the minor premise. The only way a connection is necessarily made between the two premises is for the middle term to be distributed in at least one of them.

Rule 2.  *If a term is distributed in the conclusion, it must also be distributed in its premise.* This rule is a result of the more general rule that, in a valid syllogism, the conclusion cannot go beyond the premises. If a term in the conclusion refers to all members of a particular class (i.e. the term is distributed), then the term in its premise must refer to all members of its class.

This rule can be illustrated by looking again at the example at the top of the page. In the conclusion, we have an **O** statement. By looking at our paradigm, we can see the predicate of an **O** statement is distributed. That term must therefore be distributed in the premise in which it occurs. That happens to be the major premise. The term is *men*. The term *men* is distributed in the premise, as we can see through looking at the paradigm again.

When this rule is broken it can have one of two names. If the major term is distributed in the conclusion, but not in the premise, it is known as the **Fallacy of an Illicit Major**. Predictably enough, if the minor term is distributed in the conclusion, but not in the premise, it is known as the **Fallacy of an Illicit Minor**.

Here is an example of an illicit major:

*Some rocks are granite.*
*No granite is a sandstone.*
*Therefore some sandstones are not rocks.*

You see that the major term, *rocks,* is distributed in the conclusion, but it is not distributed in its premise. So this syllogism is invalid.

Rule 3. *A valid syllogism cannot have two negative premises.* Any syllogism which has only **E** or **O** statements as premises is therefore invalid. This rule is an easy one to apply. The following combinations of premises are therefore invalid: **OO, OE, EO,** and **EE**. One of the premises must *affirm* something. If they are both negations, no valid conclusion can be drawn.

Consider the following example:

*Some Turks are not Muslims.*
*No Hindus are Muslims.*
*Therefore, some Hindus are not Turks.*

If we apply our rule, we can immediately see that the syllogism violates it. The premises are **O** and **E** statements, respectively, which are both negative.

If the rule is broken, we say that it is the **Fallacy of Two Negative Premises**.

Rule 4. *A valid syllogism cannot have a negative premise and affirmative conclusion.* The first thing to do is determine the nature of the conclusion. If it is affirmative (**A** or **I**), then it cannot have an **E** or **O** statement in the premises.

Consider this example:

*All Turks are Muslims.*
*No Hindus are Muslims.*
*Therefore, some Hindus are Turks.*

This syllogism breaks our fourth rule. The conclusion is affirmative (an **I** statement), and the minor premise is a negative premise (an **E** statement). In testing with this rule, look *first* at the conclusion. If it is affirmative, quickly scan the premises and determine if either is negative. If one is, then the syllogism is necessarily invalid.

Any syllogism which breaks this rule may be said to commit the **Fallacy of a Negative Premise and an Affirmative Conclusion.**

Rule 5. *A valid syllogism cannot have two affirmative premises and a negative conclusion.* With this rule, the means of testing is similar to the means with the fourth rule. If the conclusion is negative, then one of the premises must also be negative. For example:

> *All whales are mammals.*
> *No canaries are mammals.*
> *Therefore, some canaries are not whales.*

We see right away that the conclusion is negative. This means that at least one of the premises has to be negative as well, which the minor premise is.

Here is an example which breaks this rule:

> *All whales are sea creatures.*
> *Some sea creatures are warm-blooded animals.*
> *Therefore, no warm-blooded animals are whales.*

When this rule is broken, the syllogism makes the **Fallacy of Two Affirmative Premises and a Negative Conclusion.**

**Summary:** In testing by rule, there are five rules to keep in mind. If a syllogism breaks just one rule, it is invalid. If it passes all five, it is necessarily valid. There are two rules that involve distributed terms: the middle must be distributed in at least one premise, and if a term is distributed in the conclusion, then it must be distributed in the premise in which it occurs. The last three rules involve the quality of the statements. A valid syllogism cannot have two negative premises, it cannot have a negative premise with an affirmative conclusion, and it cannot have two affirmative premises and a negative conclusion.

## Exercise 18

In the following exercise, analyze the syllogisms. Identify which rules are violated in the syllogism by writing the name of the fallacy or fallacies. If no fallacy is made, write "valid." The premises are *not* necessarily in standard order. (Hint: the first syllogism violates three rules).

1. *Some chefs are not fat people.*
   *No fat person is a contented person.*
   *Therefore, all chefs are contented people.*   _____

2. *All water is blue liquid*
   *No blue liquid is a solid object.*
   *Therefore, some water is not a solid object.*   _____

3. *Some Christians are not Bible-readers.*
   *No Bible-reader is an ignorant person.*
   *Therefore, no ignorant person is a Christian.*   _____

4. *All Muslims are Hindus.*
   *All Hindus are Christians.*
   *Therefore, some Christians are not Muslims.*   _____

5. *No dog is a cat.*
   *Some cats are female.*
   *Therefore, some dogs are female.*   _____

6. *Some politicians are corrupt men.*
   *Some corrupt men are Mafia members.*
   *Therefore, some politicians are Mafia members.*   _____

7. *No honors students are rugby players.*
   *Some athletes are rugby players.*
   *Therefore, some athletes are not honors students.*   _____

8. *Some challenging games are not fun games.*
*Some fun games are not chess.*
*Therefore, all challenging games are chess.*            _____

9. *Some professionals are millionaires.*
*Some millionaires are not lazy men.*
*Therefore, no lazy men are professionals.*            _____

10. *Some Baptists are immersionists.*
*No Presbyterian is a Baptist.*
*Therefore some Presbyterians are not immersionists*_____

**Challenge:** For additional practice, find the fallacies made by the syllogisms in exercises 13, 16 and 17.

# ARGUMENTS IN
# NORMAL ENGLISH

## Immediate Inferences

We are now able to determine the validity of any standard-form categorical syllogism. However, most arguments we run into in daily life are expressed in normal English, rather than the more stilted categorical form. In order to make the skills we have learned more practical, we need to consider how to translate arguments in normal English into standard syllogisms. We will first look at translations resulting from immediate inferences.

An **immediate inference** is a statement which can be inferred directly from another statement. It resembles a syllogism with only one premise, and is related to the concepts of implication and equivalence.

We have already mentioned a number of immediate inferences in this text. For example, from the square of opposition we know that *Some S is P* can be immediately inferred from *All S is P* by subimplication. We also learned in the section on logical equivalence that the statements in the following sets can be immediately inferred from each other:

*No S is P ≡ No P is S*

*Some S is P ≡ Some P is S*

The immediate inference which switches the subject and predicate of a statement like this is called the **converse**.

The converse is only valid for **E** and **I** statements. **A** and **O** statements do not have a valid converse. *All S is P* does not imply that *All P is S*. If it did, then the fact that *All women are people* would imply that *All people are women*. Similarly, *Some dogs are not poodles* does not mean that *Some poodles are not dogs*.

Another type of immediate inference is the **obverse**. The obverse of a statement is obtained by changing the quality of the statement (*All* changes to *No*, *Some* to *Some...not*, and vice versa) and changing the predicate to its complement (*P* to *non-P*). Each of the four categorical statements have a valid obverse. They are translated as follows:

*All S is P ≡ No S is non-P.*

So the statement *All believers are Christians* is equivalent to *No believers are non-Christians*.

*No S is P ≡ All S is non-P.*

Thus, *No demons are atheists* means the same as *All demons are non-atheists*.

*Some S is P ≡ Some S is not non-P.*

So *Some incredible things are possible* implies that *Some incredible things are not impossible.* And finally,

*Some S is not P ≡ Some S is non-P.*

This is the most obvious. *Some Americans are not capitalists* is equivalent to *Some Americans are non-capitalists.*

The third type of immediate inference is called the **contrapositive**. The contrapositive switches the subject and predicate of **A** and **O** statements, like the converse, but it changes both subject and predicate of each to their complements. This can be derived from the other two immediate inferences. Follow the two translations closely:

| | | |
|---|---|---|
| *All S is P* | | *Some S is not P* |
| ↓ | by obverse | ↓ |
| *No S is non-P* | | *Some S is non-P* |
| ↓ | by converse | ↓ |
| *No non-P is S* | | *Some non-P is S* |
| ↓ | by obverse | ↓ |
| *All non-P is non-S* | | *Some non-P is not non-S* |

Thus the statement *All saved people are believers* is equivalent to *All non-believers are unsaved people.* Similarly, though perhaps more awkwardly, *Some faithful people are not Buddhists* translates into its contrapositive *Some non-Buddhists are not unfaithful people.*

Notice that the contrapositive is not valid for **E** and **I** statements. You can prove this by trying to put either type of statement through the translation procedure above. After the first obverse, you obtain statements which have no valid converse.

Now, consider the following argument. Is it valid or invalid?

*All non-believers are unsaved people.*
*No believers are non-Christians.*
*Therefore, all Christians are saved people.*

As it is written, this argument has six terms: *saved people, unsaved people, Christians, non-Christians, believers* and *non-believers*. It also looks as if it has a negative premise and an affirmative conclusion. But in order to analyze it for validity, we need to reduce the number of terms down to the standard three using the immediate inferences.

The major premise is an **A** statement. Thus we can take its contrapositive and change it into *All saved people are believers*. The minor premise can be changed into its obverse, *All believers are Christians*. Thus the whole argument becomes

> *All saved people are believers.*
> *All believers are Christians.*
> *Therefore, all Christians are saved people.*

This argument can now be analyzed by the techniques already covered. We see that it is an **AAA-4** syllogism, which is invalid, having an illicit minor term.

**Summary:** Immediate inferences are statements which can be inferred directly from other statements. There are three main types of immediate inferences. Converse switches the subject and predicate and is valid for **E** and **I** statements. Obverse changes both the quality of the statement and the predicate to its complement, and is valid for all statements. Contrapositive switches the subject and predicate of the statement and changes both to their complements; It is valid for **A** and **O** statements.

## Exercise 19

Write two valid immediate inferences for each of the statements given. Identify the immediate inferences as either *converse*, *obverse*, or *contrapositive*.

1. All things that glitter are gold.

_____

_____

2. No emperors were philosophers.

_____

_____

3. Some prophets are pagans.

_____

_____

4. Some mathematicians are not teachers.

_____

_____

Now translate the following arguments into standard-form categorical syllogisms. Note that they may not be in proper order. Also, find and identify the one invalid syllogism.

5. Some Christians are Calvinists, but no Christians are unbelievers. Therefore some Calvinists are believers.

6. All mumbling is murmuring, so all mumbling is nonsensical, since no murmuring is sensical.

7. All perfect beings are nonhuman, since all mortals are imperfect, and no humans are immortals.

8. All eighth graders are less than six-feet tall, because all poor logicians are non-eighth graders, and nobody six feet tall or more is a good logician.

9. Some non-adults are not immature people, but no mature people are impatient people. We must conclude that some adults are patient people.

10. No things that glitter are non-gold, and all gold is expensive. Thus, nothing that glitters is inexpensive.

## Translating Ordinary Statements

Categorical statements are given in very formal language, but in everyday arguments they can be expressed in a wide variety of ways. You have already done some translation of ordinary statements into categorical form, but many more means of expressing statements need to be considered.

For example, we have already learned that categorical form requires verbs to be changed into nouns. Thus the ordinary statement *All roads lead to Rome* gets translated into *All roads are to-Rome leaders.*

Similarly, we have seen that, for proper categorical form, adjectives must become nouns. We reject *All toads are ugly* as categorical form. It must be translated into something like *All toads are ugly amphibians.*

The assignments have also required you to recognize some synonyms to the words *all, no* and *some.* The following are some examples:

*All* — every, any, as many as

*No* — none, all...not, never

*Some* — many, most, a few

Note that statements starting *Not all...* should be translated *Some... not.* Thus, *Not all students are bad* means *Some students are not bad people.*

We will now identify some additional statements in ordinary English which require more careful translation.

1. **Singular statements.** Statements often refer to a single person or thing. When they do, they are usually best translated as universals. Thus they would be changed like this:

*John is a mailman.*

*All John is a mailman.*

Singular statements which are denials are translated in the same way. For example:

*You are not my people.*

*No you are my people.*

Again, while this may sound awkward, it allows us to keep things straight.

2. **Indefinite statements**. Some statements look very similar to singular statements, but the context requires them to be translated differently. For example, consider the sentence

*Dogs ate my homework.*

This statement should not be translated *All dogs were my homework eaters*, since no doubt only a few dogs were involved. This is better changed to

*Some dogs were my homework eaters.*

Translating indefinite statements requires the student to think about the meaning of the statements in the argument. Consider this argument:

*Cats are mammals.*
*Cats sang outside my window.*
*Therefore mammals sang outside my window.*

The first statement should be translated into a universal, *All cats are mammals*. The second, however, should be translated into the particular *Some cats were outside-my-window singers*. How would you translate the conclusion?

3. **Hypothetical statements**. Many statements use *if...then...* language. We will consider this in more detail in a later section, but for now we can recognize that such statements can be translated into universals, such as

*If you like chocolate, you will love this cake.*

*All chocolate likers will be lovers of this cake.*

Similarly, negative hypotheticals can be translated into **E** statements:

*If it's a hard test then I won't pass.*

*No hard test is a test I will pass.*

We will practice with these before we look at more difficult translations.

## Exercise 20

Translate the following statements in normal English into standard categorical form.

1. God is good.

_____

2. As many as are led by the Spirit of God, these are sons of God.

_____

3. If you sin then you are a lawbreaker.

_____

4. Not everybody will come.

_____

5. A soft answer turns away wrath.

_____

6. If anyone loves the world, the love of the Father is not in him.

_____

7. Many antichrists have come.

_____

8. I believe.

_____

9. The Pharisees sit in Moses' seat.

_____

10. The love of most will grow cold.

_____

*Arguments in Normal English*

**Parameters and Exclusives**

1. **Parameters**. Some statements employ what may be called parameters. These would include question-word parameters such as *whoever, whatever, wherever, whenever, however;* time parameters like *always* and *never;* and other similar words like *who, what, where, when, how,* and *that.* Let's look at some examples.

*You should eat whatever your mother feeds you.*

The word *whatever* is a question-word parameter which is best translated *all things.* The words following the parameter are usually the subject; the remainder of the statement becomes the predicate, as follows:

*You should eat **whatever** <u>your mother feeds you</u>.*

***All things** <u>your mother feeds you</u> are things you should eat.*

Consider this use of a parameter:

*Whenever two or more of you are gathered in my name, there I shall be in the midst of you.*

Depending on the rest of the argument, this can be translated in terms of time or place. Considering the parameter *whenever,* we can translate it

*All times that two or more of you are gathered in my name are times that I will be in the midst of you.*

You need to be very careful with time parameters such as *always* and *never.* Sometimes the translation is easy:

*The poor you will always have with you.*

*All times are times the poor will be with you.*

But consider the translation of this statement:

*Joe always wins at chess.*

83

This should not be translated *All times are times Joe wins at chess*, because sometimes Joe is not playing chess. It is best translated

*All times Joe plays chess are times Joe wins at chess.*

Sometimes shorter versions of question-word parameters are used. They should be translated in the same way as their longer counterparts. In this example, the word *where* acts like the word *wherever.*

*I will go where you go.*

*All places you go are places I will go.*

Then, notice that even the word *that* can be used as a parameter. Take this statement, for example:

*All's well that ends well.*

This is best translated

*All things that end well are things that are well.*

2. **Exclusives**. Words which exclude—such as *only, unless,* and *except*—require special attention as well. We will look at one example of each. First, consider this statement:

*Only the good die young.*

What is the categorical form of this statement? Initially, you may want to translate it *All good people are people who die young.* But that is not the meaning of the statement, any more than *Only women are mothers* means *All women are mothers.* The statement is really this one:

*All people who die young are good people.*

The words *nobody but, nothing but* and so on are all translated in this same way.

Now consider this statement:

*The plants will die unless you water them.*

This does not mean that *All the plants you water are plants that do not die.* The above statement could still be true, but if you faithfully water the plant, it will still eventually die. Rather, the statement should become

*All the plants you do not water are the plants that die.*

Or, by the contrapositive,

*All the plants that do not die are the plants you water.*

Finally, the word *except* must be considered. Statements that employ *except* often contain two independent statements, which should both be considered. For example,

*Everyone was invited to the clubhouse except sisters.*

This clearly includes the following statement:

*All non-sisters were clubhouse-invited people.*

But this statement just as clearly includes the meaning

*No sisters were clubhouse-invited people.*

Obviously, the translation of arguments which use the type of statements in these last two sections requires some careful thought and practice. Often, the best approach is simply to ask, "What does this statement really mean?" If the meaning can be correctly carried across into the statements in categorical form, then the arguments can be examined for validity.

**Summary:** Arguments with statements in normal English must first be translated into categorical form in order to be examined. The last two sections have considered the translations of singular, indefinite, and hypothetical statements, and statements which employ parameters and exclusives.

## Exercise 21

Translate the following statements in normal English into standard categorical form.

1. Wherever you go, there you are.

_____

2. You may prepare it however you like.

_____

3. Unless you repent, you too will perish.

_____

4. He never did anything wrong.

_____

5. You will reap what you sow.

_____

6. He gets sick whenever he drinks milk.

_____

7. Righteousness is found only in the Lord.

_____

8. God does whatever He pleases.

_____

9. You always hurt the one you love.

_____

10. Nobody leaves except those who have finished.

_____

Translate the following arguments into standard categorical form.

11. Happy is the land that has no history, and King Frank's land has no history. We must conclude that King Frank's land is happy.

12. None but the wise are truly happy, so Solomon was happy, since he was so wise.

13. Some people are not Christ's disciples, for whoever turns away cannot be His disciple, and many people turn away.

14. All sciences except logic study the tangible, and chemistry is not logic. Thus, chemistry is a study of the tangible.

15. *Write a counterexample to the one invalid argument on this page.*

## Enthymemes

We have come a long way toward being able to analyze arguments in normal English. Still, most of the arguments that you come across in daily life do not explicitly state all of the premises, and some even leave the conclusion unstated. Arguments in which a statement is left assumed are called **enthymemes**. We must now consider how to change enthymemes into complete, standard-form syllogisms.

We will work through some examples step-by-step. Here is an argument you might hear in everyday conversation:

*You aren't invited to the party, because only eighth-graders are invited.*

First, we locate the conclusion. In this argument, the conclusion is the first statement, *You aren't invited to the party*. Translating this into categorical form gives us

*No you are invited persons.*

Second, consider the other statement, *Only eighth-graders are invited*. If we put this in standard form we obtain

*All invited persons are eighth-graders.*

We see that this has the major term, *invited persons*, so it is the major premise. Put this into proper order, and leave a space for the missing premise:

*All invited persons are eighth-graders.*

(                                   )

∴ *No you are invited persons.*

The missing premise must contain the terms that have been used only once, in this case *you* and *eighth-graders*. If the person is arguing validly, the missing premise must also be an **E** statement. Since an **E** statement is equivalent to its converse, it doesn't matter what order the terms are placed in. Thus the missing premise could be *No you are eighth-graders*, and the complete syllogism would then be

> *All invited persons are eighth-graders.*
>
> (*No you are eighth-graders.*)
>
> ∴ *No you are invited persons.*

The enthymeme has thus been translated into categorical form. It is an **AEE-2** syllogism. The missing premise was found by considering which terms were used only once in the other statements, and by considering what the quality of the statement had to be, assuming the person was arguing validly. For the sake of clarity, the assumed premise is placed in parentheses.

Consider another example, this time from the Bible. In Matthew 27:4 Judas says:

> *I have sinned, for I have betrayed innocent blood.*

What was Judas assuming in this enthymeme? First, we consider the conclusion, *I have sinned*, and put it into categorical form:

> *All I am a sinner.*

The given premise contains the minor term *I*, so it is the minor premise. We put that into categorical form and obtain:

> *All I am an innocent-blood betrayer.*

What is the assumed premise? It is the major premise, and must contain both the middle term *innocent-blood betrayer* and the major term *sinner*. Now, we should assume that he was arguing validly, if we can (sometimes no valid syllogism is possible). If so, the only valid syllogism that ends in a universal affirmative is **AAA-1**. Thus the complete argument is

> (*All innocent-blood betrayers are sinners.*)
>
> *All I am an innocent-blood betrayer.*
>
> ∴ *All I am a sinner.*

One more example should be sufficient, again from the Bible. In this enthymeme the conclusion is left assumed:

*He who receives you receives me, and he who receive me receives the one who sent me* (Matt. 10:40).

What does Jesus leave us to conclude? If we place the premises in categorical form, and in the proper order, we obtain

*All receivers of me are receivers of God.*

*All receivers of you are receivers of me.*

( ∴                                    )

Obviously, Jesus wishes us to conclude that *He who receives you receives the one who sent me*. We can translate this into proper form and place it in the syllogism, and we obtain this as the final product:

*All receivers of me are receivers of God.*

*All receivers of you are receivers of me.*

( ∴ *All receivers of you are receivers of God.* )

**Summary:** Most arguments in daily life are expressed as enthymemes. An enthymeme is a syllogism in which one statement is left assumed. The assumed statement can be determined by considering which terms were used only once in the given statements, then considering the form of the statement which would make the syllogism valid, if possible.

## Exercise 22

Translate the following enthymemes into standard-form syllogisms. Assume the enthymeme is valid, and place parentheses around the assumed statement.

1. Tomorrow is not Tuesday, therefore tomorrow we will not have a test.

2. No enthymemes are complete, so some arguments are incomplete.

3. Some young people are not rebels, since not everyone rebels as a teenager.

4. Most Russians are not capitalists, because communists are not capitalists.

5. God does whatever He pleases, and He is pleased to save sinners. So...

Do the same for these enthymemes, all taken from scripture.

6. "This man is not from God, for he does not keep the Sabbath" (John 9:16).

7. "I will fear no evil, for you are with me" (Psalm 23:4).

8. "You are worthy, our Lord and God, to receive glory . . . for you created all things" (Rev. 4:11).

9. "The promise comes by faith, so that it may be by grace" (Rom. 4:16).

10. "Here are my mother and my brothers! For whoever does the will of my Father in heaven is my brother and sister and mother" (Matt. 12:49-50).

**Challenge:** John 8:47 is a complete syllogism. Translate it into categorical form, and determine its validity.

## Hypothetical Syllogisms

As mentioned earlier, many arguments in normal English are given in the form of hypotheticals, statements using *if...then...* language. At that time we learned that the statements could be translated into universal categorical statements (**A** or **E**), and the argument then treated like other categorical syllogisms. But hypothetical syllogisms can also be examined in a manner different from categorical syllogisms.

First, we will consider what may be called **pure hypothetical syllogisms**. This form of argument employs only hypotheticals, as follows:

> *If P then Q.*
> *If Q then R.*
> *Therefore, if P then R.*

We can use the symbol $\supset$ for *if...then*. When we do, the whole argument is symbolized

$$P \supset Q$$
$$Q \supset R$$
$$\therefore P \supset R$$

This is a valid argument, which, in fact, could be translated into an **AAA-1** categorical syllogism. Here is an example of a real-life pure hypothetical syllogism:

> *If I study, then I will get good grades.*
> *If I get good grades, then my parents will be pleased.*
> *Therefore, if I study then my parents will be pleased.*

We see the hypothetical statements combine two categorical statements around an *if...then* into one new statement. The categorical statement after the *if* is called the **antecedent**, usually abbreviated *P*. The statement after the *then* is called the **consequent**, abbreviated *Q*. The antecedent of the above conclusion is *I study*, and the consequent is *My parents will be pleased*.

Some syllogisms combine hypothetical and categorical statements. These are called **mixed hypothetical syllogisms**. We will consider two valid forms of mixed hypothetical syllogisms, and two invalid forms.

The first form we will consider is called **modus ponens.** It looks like this:

*If P then Q*
*P*
*Therefore, Q*

If we put terms from real life into the argument, we could obtain this argument:

*If I study, then I will get good grades.*
*I study.*
*Therefore, I will get good grades.*

You can see that the first statement is a hypothetical statement, and the second is a categorical statement.

If this is expressed with symbols only, we can clearly see the form of modus ponens.

$P \supset Q$
$P$
$\therefore Q$

The second type of argument is called **modus tollens**. The form of argument is:

*If P then Q*
*Not Q*
*Therefore, not P*

With the same real terms we used above, the argument would be:

*If I study, then I will get good grades.*
*I did not get good grades.*
*Therefore, I did not study.*

In symbols, modus tollens would thus be:

$P \supset Q$
$\sim Q$
$\therefore \sim P$

There are also two fallacies which take a similar form to the arguments presented above. The first is the fallacy of **Asserting the Consequent**, so named because the second premise asserts the consequent of the hypothetical statement. This is how it looks.

| | | |
|---|---|---|
| *If P, then Q* | | $P \supset Q$ |
| *Q* | Or with symbols: | $Q$ |
| *Therefore, P* | | $\therefore P$ |

With terms from the real world inserted, we see a form of invalid argument which is all too familiar.

*If I study, then I will get good grades.*
*I got good grades.*
*Therefore, I studied.*

This is what is called a *non sequitur*, meaning "it does not follow." The student may have gotten good grades some other way—cheating, for example. The initial statement does not say that studying is the *only way* to good grades. There is therefore no basis for the conclusion that studying must have been the way they were obtained.

Here is a clearer cournterexample:

*If you were a gorilla, then you would have two legs.*
*You have two legs.*
*Therefore, you must be a gorilla.*

You can see that the premises are true, but the conclusion is false. Thus asserting the consequent is invalid.

The other fallacy is called **Denying the Antecedent**, because the antecedent of the hypothetical is denied in the second premise.

| | | |
|---|---|---|
| *If P, then Q* | | $P \supset Q$ |
| *Not P* | Or with symbols: | $\sim P$ |
| *Therefore, not Q* | | $\therefore \sim Q$ |

And the real life example is:

*If I study, then I will get good grades.*
*I did not study.*
*Therefore, I will not get good grades.*

This is also a *non sequitur*. You might luck out, not study, and still get good grades.

Consider this more clear counterexample:

*If you were a gorilla, then you would have two legs.*
*You are not a gorilla.*
*Therefore, you do not have two legs.*

This clearly demonstrates that denying the antecedent is invalid.

Here is a summary of the mixed hypothetical syllogisms:

|  | | |
|---|---|---|
| **VALID** | $P \supset Q$<br>$P$<br>$\therefore Q$ | $P \supset Q$<br>$\sim Q$<br>$\therefore \sim P$ |
|  | Modus Ponens | Modus Tollens |
| **INVALID** | $P \supset Q$<br>$Q$<br>$\therefore P$ | $P \supset Q$<br>$\sim P$<br>$\therefore \sim Q$ |
|  | Asserting the consequent | Denying the antecedent |

**Summary:** Hypothetical syllogisms are very common arguments in normal English. Pure hypothetical syllogisms employ only *if...then* statements. Mixed hypothetical syllogisms employ hypotheticals and categoricals. There are two valid forms of mixed hypothetical syllogism: modus ponens, and modus tollens. There are also two invalid forms: asserting the consequent, and denying the antecedent.

## Exercise 23

Analyze each of the following arguments. In the appropriate blank, write down what form of argument it is: pure hypothetical, modus ponens, modus tollens, asserting the consequent, or denying the antecedent.

1. *If you are lazy, then you will be poor. Henry is poor, and it follows that he is therefore lazy.* _____

2. *The Bible teaches that if a man is generous, then he will prosper. We know that Mike is not generous, and therefore cannot prosper.* _____

3. *If you speak too much, sin will not be absent. If sin is not absent, then it is present. Thus if you speak too much, sin is present.* _____

4. *If a ministry is of God, then it will succeed. The Mormon church is successful, and we can conclude that it is blessed by God.* _____

5. *If you are kind to the poor, then you are lending to the Lord. Paul is kind to the poor. He is therefore lending to the Lord.* _____

6. *If you visit your neighbor too much he will get sick of you. My neighbor is not sick of me, so I don't think I visit too much.* _____

7. *If you don't answer a fool according to his folly, then he will think that he is wise. Sharon did not answer him that way. He must think he is wise.* _____

8. *If a country is rebellious, it has may rulers. Argentina has had many rulers; it must be a rebellious country.* _____

9. *If a man is lawless, even his prayers are detestable. Larry is not at all a lawless man. So his prayers must not be detestable.* _____

10. *"If you are willing, you can make me clean."*
*"I am willing,"* Jesus said. *"Be clean."* _____

11. *If recycling were necessary, then it would*
*be profitable. Recycling is not yet profitable.*
*So it must not be necessary.* _____

12. *If a man gives gifts, then everyone wants to*
*be his friend. Everyone wants to be Gordon's*
*friend. Gordon must give out a lot of gifts.* _____

13. *If they receive you they receive me. If they receive*
*me, then they receive Him who sent me. So if they*
*receive you, they receive Him who sent me.* _____

14. *If I killed you, then you would be dead. I*
*promise that I will never kill you. Therefore,*
*you will never die!* _____

15. *If you flog a mocker, then the simple will learn*
*prudence. We don't flog mockers. That must*
*be why we have so many imprudent people.* _____

16. *If you are rich, then many will want to be*
*your friend. No one wants to be Jessica's friend.*
*She must not be rich.* _____

17. *If you honor the Lord with your wealth, then*
*He will bless you greatly. Mr. Spence has always*
*honored the Lord this way. He will be blessed.* _____

18. *If you fear the Lord, then you will love*
*wisdom. A man who hates wisdom must not*
*fear the Lord.* _____

19. *If you are a Christian, then you will read*
*your Bible. I know a man who reads the Bible.*
*He must be a Christian.* _____

20. *If they had belonged to us, they would*
*have remained with us. But they went out from*
*us. This showed that they did not belong to us.* _____

## Exercise 24

Analyze the following paragraph. Separate the various arguments (there are four), and determine whether they are valid or not. Identify each argument by name.

*If Paul went to Ephesus, then he wouldn't write the Ephesians a letter. But he did write them a letter, which means that he didn't go to Ephesus. But if Paul didn't go to Ephesus, then he would not have known the people there. We know, however that Paul did go to Ephesus, therefore he did know the people there. If he knew the people in Ephesus, then he would have known the saints in Colossae too. But we know that he did not know the Christians in Colossae, which means that he didn't know the Ephesians. If Paul didn't know the Ephesians, then he would have written them a letter. He wrote them a letter, and this proves that he did not know them.*

_____

_____

_____

_____

_____

_____

_____

_____

_____

# INFORMAL FALLACIES

## Fallacies of Distraction

We have seen that arguments in normal English can be analyzed and found to be valid. Many invalid arguments are also given in ordinary language, some of which are informal fallacies. Because these errors are not made by trained logicians, they will seldom come in the form of a syllogism or other structured argument. Nevertheless, the fallacies are recognizable, and have been labeled for quick identification.

There are three main types of informal fallacies:

1. Fallacies of distraction

2. Fallacies of ambiguity

3. Fallacies of form

We will first consider fallacies of distraction. Fallacies of distraction are made when someone misses the point, or draws his hearers away from the point. Here are some of them.

1. **Ipse dixit**: This is a Latin phrase meaning, "He said it himself." The fallacy is one of illegitimately appealing to an authority to settle an argument. It follows this general form:

*X* says *p*, so *p* must be true.

The Christian must be careful how he objects to this fallacy, for there are legitimate appeals to legitimate authority—the Scriptures for instance. The heart of this fallacy is an illegitimate appeal to authority.

Consider this real-life example:

*Of course there is intelligent life on other planets. My teacher said so just yesterday.*

Teachers have legitimate authority, but not concerning the existence of interplanetary life.

2. **Ad populum**: This is an appeal "to the people," or perhaps more vividly, "to the masses." This fallacy is made when an argument rests on swaying the emotions or prejudices of the crowd.

Here is an example of *ad populum*:

*The social security system must be supported, and I am sure you will support it, just as any loyal citizen would who cared about his fellow countrymen.*

This fallacy may also occur when someone urges us to join the crowd—"everybody else is doing it." Here is a common example:

*You should support candidate Smith for office. A recent poll shows him far ahead of his competitors.*

The fact that most other people support Smith does not necessarily mean that you should.

An appeal to pity or other emotions is another form of this fallacy. An older student might commit this fallacy by arguing thus:

*I deserve an A in your class. If I don't get good grades, my parents won't let me drive the car.*

The student may deserve an A, but certainly not because of his logic.

3. **Ad baculum**: Literally, this is an appeal "to the stick." It is the fallacy of the veiled threat, and usually follows this form:

If you deny *p* you will get hurt. So *p* must be true.

The threat may be very persuasive, but it does not establish the truth of the conclusion. Notice that this does not preclude all threats, such as your mother telling you to clean your room or you won't get any supper. In that case your mother is not trying to reason to a conclusion, she is simply giving a legitimate command and setting the consequences.

Another form of this fallacy is to persuade someone to do something by appealing to personal anxiety. Consider this television commercial:

*You should try our dandruff shampoo. You don't want to be ignored by the new secretary at the office because of a few white flakes on your suit!*

4. **Ad hominem**: Meaning "to the man," this is an extremely popular fallacy. It is committed whenever someone attacks the person, rather than his argument. It can follow this general form:

*X* says *p*, and *X* is bad. So *p* must be false.

For example:

*Karl Marx was a failure of a father, and therefore communism is wrong.*

Communism is wrong, but not for that reason. It is much easier to attack the person than the argument. But name-calling is not logic, and should not be treated as such.

Another form of this fallacy is called poisoning *the well*. It is committed when one's opponent is placed in a position from which he will not be believed, no matter what he says. This fallacy is made here:

*Don't listen to my opponent. He is a notorious liar who will claim that he is telling the truth, like any liar does.*

5. **Bulverism**: This fallacy is similar to *ad hominem*. It occurs when someone attempts to prove a conclusion false simply by identifying it source. It often follows this form:

You believe *p* just because you are ( fill in the blank). So *p* is false.

Bulverism was given its name by C.S. Lewis. He said, "...I have found this vice so common that I have had to invent a name for it. I call it Bulverism. Some day I am going to write the biography of its imaginary inventor, Ezekiel Bulver, whose destiny was determined at the age of five when he heard his mother say to his father —who had been maintaining that two sides of a triangle were together greater than the third— 'Oh you say that *because you are a man*.' 'At that moment,' E. Bulver assures us, 'there flashed across my opening mind the great truth that refutation is no necessary part of argument. Assume that your opponent is wrong, and then explain his error, and the world will be at your feet'" (C.S. Lewis, *God in the Dock*, page 273).

6. **Tu quoque**: Latin for, "You also," this fallacy is also related to *ad hominem*. It is the fallacy of defending yourself by pointing out that your opponent does the same thing. While this may be discomfiting to him, it is no defense of your position at all. For example:

*Russia has no right to condemn us for spying on their government. After all, how may Russian spies are lurking within our borders?*

This fallacy is easily remembered as the "You do it, too" fallacy.

7. **Ad ignorantiam**: An appeal to ignorance. This fallacy follows this general pattern.

Nobody has proven *p* to be false (or true), so *p* must be true (or false).

Of course, the absence of evidence against a particular claim is no proof of the claim itself. Here is an example of this fallacy:

*UFOs must be alien spaceships. We have never seen any report from the government offering any other satisfactory explanation.*

8. **Chronological snobbery**: This fallacy is committed when something is attacked or defended simply because of its age. It often follows this form:

*X* is old/new, therefore *X* is good/bad.

If someone were to argue that the Bible is outdated and thus should not be believed, they are committing chronological snobbery. But someone who argued that it was *true* because it was old would be equally guilty. Truth or falsity is not established by the passage of time.

Summary: Fallacies of distraction point us toward information which is irrelevant to the conclusion. There are many different forms, including *ipse dixit, ad populum, ad baculum, ad hominem, Bulverism, tu quoque, ad ignorantiam,* and chronological snobbery.

## Exercise 25

Identify the fallacy of distraction which is being made in each of the following examples.

1. Oswald must have been the lone assassin of Kennedy. Nobody has ever been able to prove any of the conspiracy theories. _____

2. Vote YES! for our schools. Don't deny children a decent education. _____

3. Santa Claus must be real. The editor of the newspaper said so. _____

4. You believe in Jesus because you were brought up in a Christian home. _____

5. We need to appropriate billions of dollars for AIDS research. Otherwise, you or someone in your family will probably get AIDS within the next ten years. _____

6. You don't believe that Genesis is to be understood literally, do you? That's a rather old-fashioned doctrine. _____

7. We should say the pledge of allegiance at our assemblies just like every other school does. _____

8. A heretic named Servetus was burned at the stake in Geneva, and John Calvin approved of it. Calvinism has to be wrong. _____

9. You can't tell me it's wrong to cheat. You've cheated before too! _____

10. Do you disagree with me when I say that mankind is corrupt? That proves that you have been corrupted already. _____

11. The senator is accused of communist activities, and there is nothing to disprove these suspicions. _____

12. *You should read this book that your boss wrote. You would not want to jeopardize your position in this company, would you?*    _____

13. *The vice-president said that potato is spelled with an "e" at the end, so it must be true.*    _____

14. *Professor Pepper thinks teachers should get paid more so they won't leave teaching for other jobs. But he's a teacher himself, so that figures.*    _____

15. *My dad tells me that I shouldn't shoplift, but I don't listen to him, because I happen to know that he stole candy from stores when he was a kid.*    _____

16. *Of course God exists. Belief in a deity is one of the most ancient concepts of man.*    _____

*Informal Fallacies*

## Fallacies of Ambiguity

Some fallacies occur, not because the information is irrelevant, but because it is ambiguous, vague, or otherwise unclear. These can all be called fallacies of ambiguity.

1. **Equivocation**: When we use words with more than one definition, we are using them *equivocally*. In an argument, it is necessary for the terms to retain the same definition throughout. When we change the meaning of our terms in mid-argument, we commit the fallacy of equivocation.

Much of our humor depends upon equivocation, but misunderstandings do also. Gordon Clark cites the example of the teenager who answered the first question from the Westminster Shorter Catechism, which asks what is the chief end of man, by saying "His head, of course."

Consider this example:

*The only rational being is man.*
*Women are not men.*
*This explains why women are so irrational.*

Formally this argument appears to be valid. But obviously the word *man* is used ambiguously, first to mean *human*, then to mean specifically *male*.

2. **Accent**: This is similar to equivocation. We commit this fallacy when we change the meaning of a sentence, not through different definitions, but through different emphases. Compare the subtly different meanings of each of the following versions of "We should not steal our neighbors car":

a. *We* should not steal our neighbor's car. (But it is fine if someone else does.)
b. We *should* not steal our neighbor's car. (But we will anyway.)
c. We should not *steal* our neighbor's car. (It is okay if we vandalize it.)
d. We should not steal our *neighbor's* car. (But the folks across town are fair game.)
e. We should not steal our neighbor's *car*. (We're after the lawn mower.)

Note that the fallacy occurs at the point of misunderstanding. We can often make a point through emphasis, but no fallacy is made until the sentence is emphasized differently, resulting in an erroneous conclusion.

3. **Amphiboly**: This fallacy results when the grammar of a sentence is such that the sentence is misunderstood. This can occur when someone is being purposely vague. For example, the Oracle of Delphi once told the Greek King Croesus that if he went to war, he would "destroy a mighty kingdom." The king was heartened and went to war, only to be defeated. When Croesus complained, he was told that he did destroy a great kingdom—his own!

This fallacy is common among newspaper headlines and advertisements which, in an attempt to be brief, are unintentionally ambiguous. One such headline ran:

*Tuna biting off Washington coast*

If someone were to conclude that they must grow big fish in those waters, they would be committing the fallacy of amphiboly.

4. **Composition**: A fallacy of composition occurs when someone assumes that what is true of the parts must be true of the whole.

For example, if chlorine is a poison, and it is, and sodium is a poison, and it is, then if we combine them (NaCl), the result should be twice as poisonous, right? Wrong. We are talking about table salt.

Here is another example:

*Each part of the 747 airplane is designed to be lightweight. So a 747 must not weigh very much.*

5. **Division**: This is the opposite of composition. The fallacy of division is therefore made when one assumes that what is true of the whole must be true of each of the individual parts.

Here is an example:

*The Lakers are a great basketball team, so each member of the team must be a great basketball player.*

**Summary:** Fallacies of ambiguity occur when an argument is unclear. This can be due to the lack of clarity of individual words or of the sentence as a whole. We considered five types: equivocation, accent, amphiboly, composition, and division.

## Exercise 26

Name the fallacies of ambiguity being made in the following examples.

1. Mother, you told me not to take any cookies.
I didn't *take* them anywhere, I ate them right here. _____

2. *Super Frosted Sugar Bombs* must be nutritious,
because they are part of this nutritious breakfast. _____

3. My friend said that he hit his head on a rock,
breaking it into a million pieces. But I don't think
anyone could live with a shattered head! _____

4. Teacher: "I instructed you to write a letter to
someone, and you haven't done it." Student:
"Yes I did. I wrote the letter *A*." _____

5. Jesus taught that we should love our *neighbor*.
So it's okay to hate the people across town. _____

6. If two teaspoons of sugar make this taste good,
then four will make it taste twice as good! _____

7. Bread and water is better than nothing, but
nothing is better than a steak dinner. So bread
and water is better than a steak dinner. _____

8. American Indians are disappearing. But that
man is an American Indian, so he must be
disappearing, too! _____

9. I read on the front page, "Grandmother of
Eight Makes Hole in One." Her poor grandchild! _____

10. "Mary had a little lamb." I'll bet the doctor was
surprised. _____

**Fallacies of form**

Fallacies of form are arguments with a structural problem. Thus an informal argument can be invalid because of improper form like a formal argument can. Let's see how.

1. **Petitio principii**: In English, this means "begging the question." It is also called *circular reasoning*. Someone who commits this fallacy is guilty of assuming what must be proven. In other words, one of his premises already contains the conclusion, though usually in disguise.

Petitio principii follows this basic form:

*p* is true, therefore *p* is true.

Suppose you hear someone arguing that rock music is better than classical music because classical music is not as good. Bach would not be impressed with the reasoning.

But most examples of *petitio principii* are not so glaring. Consider this one, for instance:

*She must love me, because she says she does. And she would not lie to someone she loves, would she?*

Note: Some instances of circular reasoning are not necessarily fallacious. When trying to defend the truth of our ultimate standards, we find that we must beg the question. For believers, the ultimate standard is the Bible. So when a Christian apologist argues that the Bible is true because it is from God, as the Bible declares, he is simply demonstrating the Bible to be his absolute standard. An unbelieving scientist might also appeal to science to prove that science is true. This merely shows what his ultimate standard is.

2. **Post hoc ergo propter hoc**: This is Latin for "after this, therefore because of this." It is also called *false cause*. This fallacy is committed by the rooster who thought the sun rose because of his crowing. After all, every morning after he crowed, the sun rose. *Post hoc* thus follows this pattern:

*P* happened before *Q*, therefore *P* caused *Q*.

This is an easy error to fall into, particularly for over simplistic historians. The American War for Independence happened after the Renaissance, therefore the Renaissance was one of the causes. It may have been, but chronological sequence itself does not establish the fact.

3. **Either/or**: This is the fallacy of oversimplifying the choices. It is also called *bifurcation*. The one guilty of the fallacy presents a false dilemma; you must believe *either* this *or* that. There may be other options, and if there are, this fallacy is present.

Here is an example:

*What, you didn't finish your homework? You must be either stupid or lazy.*

Obviously, there could be other reasons. The questioner has assumed something which he should not before making this conclusion.

4. **Complex question**: This is the error committed when a question is framed in such a way as to exclude a legitimate response. It is also called a *loaded question*. For example, suppose a man were asked,

*Have you stopped beating your wife yet?*

To say *yes* is to admit past guilt, and to say *no* is to continue unrepentant. This fallacy is thus related to *either/or*. In both cases, something unstated is being assumed which causes a fallacy. The fallacy occurs at the point that an erroneous conclusion is drawn when the question is answered, as shown here:

*Lawyer: "What did you do with the money you stole?"*
*Witness: "Nothing!"*
*Lawyer: "Aha! So you admit to stealing the money!"*

5. **Apriorism**: This is the fallacy of the hasty generalization. We have to use the word "hasty" because generalizations can be used legitimately. We call a legitimate generalization *induction*. But if the generalization is obviously a wild leap into the void, it can be identified as the fallacy of apriorism.

For example, this little girl generalizes too quickly:

*I tried to talk to that new boy Tommy yesterday, and he stuck his tongue out at me. Boys are so mean!*

113

Do not confuse apriorism with composition. Someone who commits apriorism may look at *one* particular case, and fallaciously apply what he sees to the whole. But someone who commits the fallacy of composition looks at *all* the parts, and says what is true of them all must be true of the whole.

**Summary:** Fallacies of form result when an argument is put together in an improper way. We looked at five fallacies of form: *petitio principii, post hoc ergo propter hoc,* either/or, complex question, and apriorism.

## Exercise 27

### Identify the following fallacies of form by name.

1. *My mom wouldn't take me to the movies, and she wouldn't let me watch a video. She never wants me to have any fun.*  _____

2. *President Schwartz was just elected, and the stock market soared to new heights. I'm glad I voted for him.*  _____

3. *"Have you stopped getting drunk all the time?" "No!" "Oh, so you admit to being a drinker!"*  _____

4. *Rotten Banana is a great band. I know, because all the cool kids like them. Which are the cool kids? The ones who like Rotten Banana, of course!*  _____

5. *That guy from the community church reads all the time. They must all be bookworms out there.*  _____

6. *If you leave the Christian school, then you will have to go to the public schools.*  _____

7. *I didn't study because I had to go to church. I got an A on the test anyway. I'm going to go to church before tests more often.*  _____

8. *Miracles don't happen because that would violate natural law, and natural law cannot be violated.*  _____

9. *She killed the wicked witch of the east. So she must either be a good witch, or a bad witch.*  _____

10. *Ever since I started eating seaweed with my meals, I haven't gotten sick once. You should eat it, too!*  _____

## Detecting Fallacies

We have seen numerous informal fallacies, some of which are harder to identify than others. Recognizing fallacies as they occur in daily life (such as those found in the editorial page of most newspapers) can be even more difficult. You may have read a fallacious argument in a letter to the editor and said to yourself, "I know that's not true. I wish I could tell what is really wrong with this line of thought." How do you figure it out?

The technique for identifying informal fallacies is the same as identifying any kind of reasoning. You must ask two questions about the person doing the arguing:

1. What is he trying to prove?

2. How is he trying to prove it?

For example, consider this section out of Bertrand Russell's essay entitled *Why I am not a Christian*:

> *Religion is based, I think, primarily and mainly on fear. It is partly the terror of the unknown and partly, as I have said, the wish to feel that you have kind of an elder brother who will stand by you in all your troubles and disputes. Fear is the basis of the whole thing—fear of the mysterious, fear of defeat, fear of death.*

Now, what is Lord Russell trying to prove? He is trying to prove that Christianity is not true (consider the title of the essay). How is he trying to prove that in this paragraph? We see him attempting to identify the source of Christian faith. Apparently, he thinks that if he can say *why* someone believes Christianity, then it must not be true. Having answered these questions, we can readily spot this as an extended Bulverism.

We will do one more practice exercise identifying fallacies. As you work through them, ask yourself the two questions above. Your answers should guide you to identifying the correct fallacy.

Also, keep in mind that some bad arguments can commit more than one fallacy at a time. If you cannot decide between two possible fallacies, it may be that either one (or both) is correct.

## Exercise 28

Identify the fallacies made in the examples below. They can be any of the fallacies of distraction, ambiguity, or form.

1. The chain letter read, "If you don't keep this letter going, you may lose your job, get in an accident, or go bald!" _____

2. That chain letter was real. Just a week after I threw it away, I failed my logic test. _____

3. My girlfriend always keep chain letters going. She says that nobody has proven to her that they don't really work. _____

4. A recycling poster said, "Recycle cans and waste paper," so I am wasting paper every chance I get! _____

5. All my friends recycle their cans, so it must be a good thing to do. _____

6. I read that "Life is either a daring adventure, or nothing." My life certainly isn't a daring adventure, so I guess it's nothing. _____

7. The apostle Paul told us to honor our leaders. But he dishonored the high priest, so why should I listen to him? _____

8. Honoring your leaders is an old tradition that no longer applies to our modern, sophisticated age. _____

9. The Japanese always score higher on math than the Americans. So I am sure our Japanese neighbor can help you with your calculus. _____

10. The Japanese are better at math because they're smarter. We know that they're smarter, because they always do better at math. _____

117

11. Hi, I am selling tickets to the policeman's ball, and I am sure you would like to support your local police, so will it be cash, check or credit card? _____

12. Of course the Joint-Chiefs-of-Staff say we ought to increase military spending. As members of the armed forces, they want as much as they can get. _____

13. We shouldn't listen to Senator Slug either, since we all know he is a card-carrying member of the radical right. _____

14. Oh, so you believe in evolution? Tell me, are you descended from a monkey on your mother's side or your father's side? _____

15. The world was not created by God, for matter has always existed, and thus needs no God to explain where it came from. _____

16. The press has a duty to publish what is clearly in the public interest. And there is certainly public interest in the private life of the rich and famous. _____

17. I had a bad time with my former husband. Trust me deary, men are no good. _____

18. The idea of trying to colonize Mars is ridiculous. My mother said it couldn't possibly work. _____

19. Each snowflake is very light. There is no way that snow could make that roof collapse. _____

20. Did that last guy say snowflakes were *light* ? I always thought that snow was f*rozen water.* _____

**Challenge**: Find and identify some informal fallacies from books, newspaper articles, headlines, or even comic strips.

## Appendix

### The 256 forms of syllogisms

| | | | | | | | |
|---|---|---|---|---|---|---|---|
| AAA-1 | AAA-2 | AAA-3 | AAA-4 | IAA-1 | IAA-2 | IAA-3 | IAA-4 |
| AAE-1 | AAE-2 | AAE-3 | AAE-4 | IAE-1 | IAE-2 | IAE-3 | IAE-4 |
| AAI-1 | AAI-2 | AAI-3 | AAI-4 | IAI-1 | IAI-2 | IAI-3 | IAI-4 |
| AAO-1 | AAO-2 | AAO-3 | AAO-4 | IAO-1 | IAO-2 | IAO-3 | IAO-4 |
| | | | | | | | |
| AEA-1 | AEA-2 | AEA-3 | AEA-4 | IEA-1 | IEA-2 | IEA-3 | IEA-4 |
| AEE-1 | AEE-2 | AEE-3 | AEE-4 | IEE-1 | IEE-2 | IEE-3 | IEE-4 |
| AEI-1 | AEI-2 | AEI-3 | AEI-4 | IEI-1 | IEI-2 | IEI-3 | IEI-4 |
| AEO-1 | AEO-2 | AEO-3 | AEO-4 | IEO-1 | IEO-2 | IEO-3 | IEO-4 |
| | | | | | | | |
| AIA-1 | AIA-2 | AIA-3 | AIA-4 | IIA-1 | IIA-2 | IIA-3 | IIA-4 |
| AIE-1 | AIE-2 | AIE-3 | AIE-4 | IIE-1 | IIE-2 | IIE-3 | IIE-4 |
| AII-1 | AII-2 | AII-3 | AII-4 | III-1 | III-2 | III-3 | III-4 |
| AIO-1 | AIO-2 | AIO-3 | AIO-4 | IIO-1 | IIO-2 | IIO-3 | IIO-4 |
| | | | | | | | |
| AOA-1 | AOA-2 | AOA-3 | AOA-4 | IOA-1 | IOA-2 | IOA-3 | IOA-4 |
| AOE-1 | AOE-2 | AOE-3 | AOE-4 | IOE-1 | IOE-2 | IOE-3 | IOE-4 |
| AOI-1 | AOI-2 | AOI-3 | AOI-4 | IOI-1 | IOI-2 | IOI-3 | IOI-4 |
| AOO-1 | AOO-2 | AOO-3 | AOO-4 | IOO-1 | IOO-2 | IOO-3 | IOO-4 |
| | | | | | | | |
| EAA-1 | EAA-2 | EAA-3 | EAA-4 | OAA-1 | OAA-2 | OAA-3 | OAA-4 |
| EAE-1 | EAE-2 | EAE-3 | EAE-4 | OAE-1 | OAE-2 | OAE-3 | OAE-4 |
| EAI-1 | EAI-2 | EAI-3 | EAI-4 | OAI-1 | OAI-2 | OAI-3 | OAI-4 |
| EAO-1 | EAO-2 | EAO-3 | EAO-4 | OAO-1 | OAO-2 | OAO-3 | OAO-4 |
| | | | | | | | |
| EEA-1 | EEA-2 | EEA-3 | EEA-4 | OEA-1 | OEA-2 | OEA-3 | OEA-4 |
| EEE-1 | EEE-2 | EEE-3 | EEE-4 | OEE-1 | OEE-2 | OEE-3 | OEE-4 |
| EEI-1 | EEI-2 | EEI-3 | EEI-4 | OEI-1 | OEI-2 | OEI-3 | OEI-4 |
| EEO-1 | EEO-2 | EEO-3 | EEO-4 | OEO-1 | OEO-2 | OEO-3 | OEO-4 |
| | | | | | | | |
| EIA-1 | EIA-2 | EIA-3 | EIA-4 | OIA-1 | OIA-2 | OIA-3 | OIA-4 |
| EIE-1 | EIE-2 | EIE-3 | EIE-4 | OIE-1 | OIE-2 | OIE-3 | OIE-4 |
| EII-1 | EII-2 | EII-3 | EII-4 | OII-1 | OII-2 | OII-3 | OII-4 |
| EIO-1 | EIO-2 | EIO-3 | EIO-4 | OIO-1 | OIO-2 | OIO-3 | OIO-4 |
| | | | | | | | |
| EOA-1 | EOA-2 | EOA-3 | EOA-4 | OOA-1 | OOA-2 | OOA-3 | OOA-4 |
| EOE-1 | EOE-2 | EOE-3 | EOE-4 | OOE-1 | OOE-2 | OOE-3 | OOE-4 |
| EOI-1 | EOI-2 | EOI-3 | EOI-4 | OOI-1 | OOI-2 | OOI-3 | OOI-4 |
| EOO-1 | EOO-2 | EOO-3 | EOO-4 | OOO-1 | OOO-2 | OOO-3 | OOO-4 |